Sales Is a Team Sport

Sales Is a Team Sport

Aligning the Players With the Playbook

John Fuggles

BUSINESS EXPERT PRESS
Leader in applied, concise business books

Sales Is a Team Sport: Aligning the Players With the Playbook

First published in 2022 by
Business Expert Press, LLC
222 East 46th Street, New York, NY 10017
www.businessexpertpress.com

ISBN-13: 978-1-63742-292-2 (paperback)
ISBN-13: 978-1-63742-293-9 (e-book)

Business Expert Press Selling and Sales Force Management Collection

First edition: 2022

10 9 8 7 6 5 4 3 2 1

To my wife and my daughter.
For their encouragement and support.

Description

We see teamwork in every sphere of business, so why should sales be any different?

Sales is a critical part of any business, whether for survival or to grow and scale. Often salespeople are seen as independent hunters and farmers, but that would be wrong. Salespeople may be the tip of the spear when it comes to winning business, but great sales success is built on teamwork.

This book sets out to identify the key components and helps the reader understand what it takes to build the best team from people, skills, processes, technology, and systems. Broken down into chapters that cover everything from the sales process and managing opportunities, to the important role played by marketing, and why CRM is not just software.

Sales is a team sport. Like all team sports there are those that play on the field and those that work to help the team perform. In any organization everyone plays a part. In the field of sales, understanding how this all comes together will not only help any company, but also anyone that reads the book and wants to get more out of their role, or move their business forward and achieve greater sales success as a team.

The book is filled with personal anecdotes and real-life examples from the author's career in sales.

The author also provides regular updates and more opportunities to learn via the book's website: https://www.salesisateamsport.net/

Keywords

sales; selling; closing; funnel; sales funnel; buyer; challenger; conceptual selling; customer centric selling; Ansoff matrix; Boston Consulting Matrix; McKinsey Matrix; CAGE distance framework; Maslow hierarchy of needs; 4Ps; 7Ps; marketing mix; content marketing matrix; CRM; CRM systems; data; analytics; customers; renewals; referrals; opportunities;

marketing; project; process; negotiating; play hard; coach; players; social selling; sport; team; task/team/individual; budgeting; forecasting; success; learning; failure; winback; anecdotes; stories; examples; winning; win; win-win; contracts; cross-sell; upsell; lose; customer satisfaction; CSAT; NPS; customer loyalty; product lifecycle; market life cycle; management; tools; systems; process; implementation; support; channel management; winning team

Contents

Preface

When I talk to colleagues, friends, and associates about sales and about how to build a sales team and what that means, it often surprises me that what seems obvious to me is less so to those who have not been at the sharp end of sales. We all have within us so much that we know that we assume everyone else also knows.

I have worked in sales, most of my working life as a salesperson, leading a sales team, or in a consultative capacity. In that time, I have come to understand what makes great salespeople and what makes a great sales team and, more importantly you can have one without the other, but it won't last or won't be as successful.

Encouraged by my wife I thought about writing a book. I mentioned the idea to two friends, both of whom have achieved high status in their careers. The response was the same, both had learned much from our conversations over the years and both felt I should share that understanding more widely.

Researching the book was as enjoyable as writing. Delving back into books I had not read for some time to read again and finding new books to learn from. Only a handful of these are credited within my book but, to all those not mentioned, thank you for your contribution.

I hope the reader enjoys the anecdotes and takes forward new thoughts and ideas they can develop and make their own. If sales is a team sport, then the coaches need a coaching manual. I hope this forms part of your coaching manual, whether for yourself or for your team.

Acknowledgments

All the great salespeople and sales managers I have had the opportunity to work with and all those that have worked for me and impressed me with their sales skills. I have learned something from them all and am still learning.

Introduction

Sales IS a Team Sport

The best teams are built with individuals who work together for a common purpose and are willing to sacrifice for the good of the team. Not seeking personal glory. Great teams are built when *"the whole is greater than the sum of its parts"* (Aristotle). This applies to any field of play and, in business, the field where you play is the battleground on which business is won.

Winning does not happen immediately. Getting the right team together to support each other and to win takes time. Even with the best team there is no guarantee; it still takes effort, practice and occasionally, more changes to the team or the starting line-up.

At their height, the *Chicago Bulls* had Michael Jordan to lead the team, but ably assisted by Scottie Pippen and Horace Grant both of whom joined the Bulls in 1987. Jordan joined the *Chicago Bulls* in 1984 but never won the championship until 1991. It took four years after the team was assembled for the results to come. Even with the best players and the best supporting players winning does not happen immediately.

The world of sport is littered with great teams and great individuals that never won their ultimate prize. Winning is about fine margins, attention to detail and great individuals, perhaps not always the best, and the will to win. One great player may win the occasional spoil but it is not sustainable.

George Best was, at the time, one of the best football players in the world. Despite many challenges his touch on the pitch was legendary, as was his personal life. In 1968, Best was awarded the title European Footballer of the Year, yet throughout his entire 37 caps for his country they never once qualified for the European Championships nor for the World Cup of Football.

The best teams very often have some great players and star performers but one individual stand-out player who disrupts the team or tries to work alone may be fine for a short period but is not sustainable and may lead to others leaving the team.

In U.S. Basketball, we think of great players and the impact they had, but sometimes it is not always the positive impact that brings results or causes damage to the team. Between 2005 and 2008, the *Washington Wizards* made it to the Play-offs. Gilbert Arenas and Javaris Crittenton were part of the 2008/2009 team and both keen gamblers. A locker room incident in 2009, where they argued over gambling debts, and both drew guns on each other, had a huge impact. Both were suspended and one never played in the *NBA* again. After both players were suspended, the *Wizards* lost more games than they won and never returned to the play-offs until 2014.

It is not just how you play to win as an individual within the team. It is who you are and how you react and work with your colleagues and associates. Sales is a team sport, and it matters that the individuals within the team work together both in the sales pursuit and more widely as a team.

But all teams need a way to play. We call this the Sales Process. The tools you need are called Systems, such as presentation tools, competitor analysis sheets, Customer Relationship Management (CRM) systems and reporting. Working together for the common goal requires understanding of what tactics work and what needs more work, what needs to be changed and even if some of the team members need to be changed.

My boss came to talk to me about an existing account we had within the company. The salesperson working the account had been on it for a year and had managed to retain the business but had not grown the account or secured much in the way of wins.

The Sales Manager went to see the Chief Operating Officer of the company to find out why and wanted the client to be completely open. Not only did the COO feel the salesperson was too focused on his product and not on the needs of the customer he also did not like him personally.

We all accept that business should be about what you do, what value add you bring and your contribution more than your personality. However, we are all human beings, and we are sociable animals, which means sometimes we get on with people, sometimes not. Whether a personality clash had got in the way of a productive partnership, or the different approaches led to the clash should not matter, because it was not working for either party.

The sales Account Manager on the account was changed and I inherited an account that was seen as going nowhere. In truth it grew very little as opportunities were sparse but on a personal level the relationship progressed and the cost of serving the account in terms of time and effort reduced so there was a win there too.

Sometimes the team is not just the team within. The team that is the client account and the sales team itself must also work as a partnership.

In John Adair's book, *The Action Centred Leadership* we have become used to seeing Task–Team–Leadership as the three elements of great leadership. These same principles apply to sales and how to build an effective sales program in any business. The task is easily the sales pursuit and all that goes with that to win the deal. The team and individual come together to win. And this is shown in Figure I.1.

There are a myriad of books on sales and sales techniques, sales methodologies, and sales skills development. Type "sales techniques" in amazon.com and you have over 60,000 results to choose from. Different markets and industries require different approaches and skill sets. Selling an Airbus to a national carrier is somewhat different to selling photocopiers

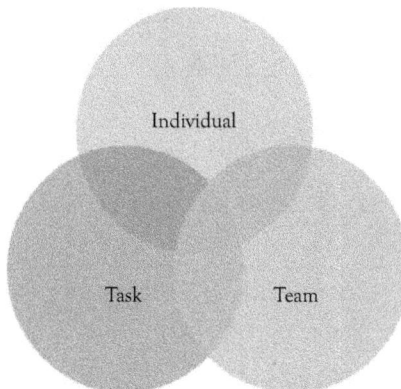

Figure I.1 The three elements of Action Centered Leadership

to a small office. Accepted there are many common elements, but there are more differences in the style, the approach, the level of detail, the size of the team, the duration, and much more besides. However, both require a team, and both have a task to complete.

Team building can be simple and yet very effective, such as an evening out or trip to the beach. It does not have to be a three-day wilderness adventure and raft-building. However, it is widely recognized that team building within a business is important; so it should also follow that team building within the sales team is important. Very often this is confined just to the sales team. It would be better for a wider team to be involved in team building, the marketing team, and those that are actively engaged in supporting the sales process and the pursuit of the sale.

Putting together the elements required of an organization to build an effective sales engine requires an understanding of the task in detail and the tools and systems to support that. It requires great players and ones that can work as part of a team. Bringing that all together will deliver sustainable, repeatable wins and allow the company to continue developing and tuning their product or service and the way they go about the sales pursuit to even better results.

CHAPTER 1

The Sales Process

Overview

Sales is a process. It has no start, it has no end, it just keeps going around and around. But the sales process lets fly opportunities, some call pursuits, sometimes engagements or just plainly "a sale." These are not part of the process but are driven by the process whether that is your process, or the process dictated by the customer, such as in a competitive tender situation. The sales pursuit should be thought of more as a project.

In this chapter, we will address the different approaches for existing or lapsed customers and how to identify and engage new conversations with potential clients of the future. Knowing how to win over new customers and how to demonstrate your value to existing customers are all part of the sale. Often, we separate New Business Development as a role from Account Management as a role. While there are many differences and there are some different skill sets required, there is still considerable overlap in how salespeople engage and control the conversation and how salespeople remain focused on the prize they are seeking. Lose focus on the ultimate objective and you cease to be a salesperson.

We will look at the Sales Funnel. There are many variations to the funnel, but they all hold the same truth. How to manage many interests at the start to a deal at the end. How to sift and sort and manage multiple pursuits to increase the chance of backing the winning horse every time.

We will look at the difference between sales as a process and sales as a single pursuit, or project; how to manage each of these Opportunities. A keyword search throws up some, perhaps, surprising results. The Market and The Process are significant elements of the sale. In sales, salespeople often see processes as filling in CRM updates or box ticking to satisfy a report, but for great salespeople Process is a vital tool to retain focus and ensure consistent progress toward the goal.

The most exciting part of any sale should be when the customer has a pen in hand and a document in front of them. Today perhaps there is much less theater as remote selling, plus electronic documents, and signatures, have replaced much of that. However, until that signature appears, it is not a sale, it is not real, it is just an idea that the salesperson, and the customer, want to realize.

In this chapter, we will look briefly at what happens after signature, toward implementation and post go-live support. Sales may be about winning but great salespeople are about much more than that. They are about process, control, they are about focus and dogged determination. The parallels between top athletes and top salespeople are many and those that play as part of a team focus not only on the game at hand but the future of the team and the season long after they have retired from the field of play.

What Is the Sales Process?

The Sales Process is one part of a system. It has component parts such as the Sales Funnel, the Pipeline, and works in parallel with CRM systems or perhaps Opportunity Tracking Systems (OTS) and then has wrapped around its skills, tools, techniques, data, products, and, of course, people. When all is considered, a Sales Process is not so much a fast jet rather a load of nuts and bolts flying in close formation. It may not always be joined up, but these individual parts do seem to serve a common purpose and work together.

According to Customer Centric Selling, the sales process is *"a defined set of repeatable, interrelated activities from market awareness through servicing customers that allows communication progress to date to others within the company."*

Diagrams of a sales process are either a linear chart or a circle. Accepting it is a process, the cyclical design makes more sense. What is often drawn is not so much the process but the hub of an altogether more complex series of processes and procedures leading to projects. Even before the process starts, there is work to be done. In much the same way that games are often won and lost long before the team gets on the pitch. But let us start with the basics.

Some leads will be new and may have been acquired, they called you or you called them—"cold calling"—to qualify them as a potential customer. Other leads will be of or from existing accounts or from existing contacts. So, let us start there.

Existing Customers

Existing customers we should also include lapsed customers and long-standing contacts or companies that have never been customers. Accepted they are not customers but the journey to make them a customer begins at the same point.

A company that already buys a product or service from you is a great place to start. We can sell them more stuff (one of my all-time favorite words) and, if we do not have anything new to sell them, we can always find a way to expand our portfolio or develop additional offerings that may appeal.

Simply picking up the phone and telling a customer you have something new for them to buy is unlikely to win new business, or rather it may but only on the rarest of occasions. Sales is about managing the process, implementing the sales pursuit, and winning the deal. But, for existing customers, at least we have a relationship as a good place to start. Even if the customer is not happy with your current product or service you at least have insight into their business and can turn a poor performance to your advantage.

In the same way that we learn more from our failures than we do success, a company that is experiencing difficulties with your product or service will also see how you work to resolve it. They too will learn more from your failures than your success. That is not to say you should set out to fail! But it does mean you can take a bad situation and gain from it in the long run.

I remember my first meeting with the Chief Information Officer of a very well-known shipping company. I arrived at his office, some three hours' drive from home, looking forward to our first meeting. He was an established account with my company, but I was new in the role.

I was kept waiting a long time in the reception area. My first thought was that he was putting into place some powerplay, letting me know he was the boss. Eventually I was ushered to the lift, through the IT department and into his office. His first comment: "Don't sit down, you're not staying long."

I was knocked back, that certainly was some powerplay, he was expecting me to stand there while he ruled over me from behind a very large desk in an equally large office.

What he said next explained everything. While I had been making my way to their office his entire data network had crashed. He had no way of sharing shipping manifests, cargo details and all other pieces of critical data to his ports and to the authorities. The reason he had not called in advance to tell me was lost and the reason my office never called me is still unknown to this day.

I left his office, went to the nearest empty desk, and sat down. I immediately set to work, finding out what happened, organizing resources, working out alternative fixes, and keeping on top of matters. None of this was my responsibility and, in truth, there was little I could do to influence the course of events.

As the network came back up, bit by bit, I made sure I was always fully informed. As we were about 80% there I walked back into Chris' office. Not knocking and not waiting for his PA to show me in.

"Okay, as of right now we have 80% up and working" and gave a short but accurate description of what we had achieved and the believed cause of the issue. This was my powerplay. I showed the CIO that I was in command of his account. I chose not to knock because I knew how important this was and I wanted to demonstrate my understanding of the situation in my manner as much as the information I delivered.

I looked after that account for about another two years. Chris and I met every Friday morning, he made the coffee, and I brought the donuts. As an account we lapped up every order and grew the revenues several-fold.

What won the day was how my company responded and, equally importantly, how I "took control"—or at least that was the perception I created. My command of the situation and direct approach showed Chris I was someone he could rely on and my company would work doubly hard when there was an issue.

As a customer you only get to see the true commitment of a supplier when things go wrong. Taking ownership, accepting failings, and going beyond the outcome expectations of the customer will put you in a favorable light. But, be warned, failing, and reacting too slowly will not help. Making the same mistake more than once is also not acceptable in most Executives' eyes too.

Within an existing account there will often be personnel changes over time. It is important to keep good contact at different levels and across the organization to build lasting relationships. Think of any client as a matrix, make sure you have width in your coverage and depth within the key departments.

There is no point having the Executives onside if the people tasked with implementing and running what it is you sold simply refuse to use it. Similarly winning the backing of the team required to run a system is not going to help if the Executives do not know about you. Likewise having one department backing you, even if it is the Procurement Department, is not the best recipe for success either.

There are many systems and courses that will help you navigate your way through complex organizations and give you the multiple touch points that result in the stickiness you need. Once won, this is account management. For accounts not yet won, this is good sales opportunity management.

For larger sales organizations, new business sales and existing account management are often separated. They not only require many of the same skills but also require different skills and approaches. For existing accounts, it becomes more important to understand the nature of the relationships and nurture them for future growth. Identifying the next sales opportunity with an established bridgehead is different to selling the first product or solution to a new account.

For existing accounts, it is important to maintain a healthy relationship with your client. Healthy does not mean pandering to the client. Having the business conversations that allow you the insight into their plans is important. Able to have an open dialogue and, at times, very honest exchanges will stand in good stead for the long term. That does not mean you have to play golf with them and take them to bars and restaurants just to curry favor. Indeed, too much of this and it can become tiring, confusing, conflicting and, possibly even in breach of laws and regulations.

Business relationships are just that. They are business but they are also a relationship. Getting to know what football team your contact supports or what is their favorite pastime can be useful. Use it to your advantage but do not overplay the hand.

Under various anti-bribery laws, accepting of gifts has now become something that requires company sign-off, particularly if the gift has a high price tag associated. In many countries there are limits to the value amount that can be accepted. Note, however, in many such regulations there is an exception for "local custom" and some people may even be exempt from the regulations.

Take something as simple as a round of golf at your local club. Invite some of your customers, perhaps to a tournament with other customers and partners. What about those that do not play golf? What about those that do but you have no room to invite? What if a competitor of theirs trounces them on the greens? Not forgetting it also means they get, in effect, a day off work. Sometimes the rub of the green is not out on the links but back in the office.

The CIO of a large organization and client of mine was a keen cricketer and loyal Australian. His right-hand-man was Indian and very keen on supporting his nation in the upcoming ICC Cricket World Cup.

I had organized for myself and a colleague to take us all to one of the Cricket World Cup semi-finals. Australia and India: one of them was bound to make the semi-finals; so it seemed like a good idea. The match was in Edgbaston, so we had a couple of hours on the train to get there, and after an evening meal, the last train back.

What we saw was New Zealand versus Pakistan. My work colleague spent the entire day—and for several days before and many after—laughing hysterically at how my plans had been completely undone. On the day we had the "Ozzie" cheering on Pakistan and the "Kiwis" being supported by a chap from India!

The customer took note to regularly remind me of the event. Even after they stopped being a client I kept in touch, and it became folklore. In truth it worked better that the two wrong teams were playing that had it been Australia versus India!

Entertaining clients is an opportunity to find new and common ground. It need not be taken too seriously and whatever the outcome it should always leave a positive impression. In my case I did become the butt of the joke, but it still served as a great way to build a relationship, arguably more so as a result of what happened.

It is only natural that we get on better with some people more than we do others. Now imagine if you do not particularly like your customer—or if they do not like you!

The occasional social event may be a good idea and being creative is often seen as a better idea than blowing the budget. Some of the best customer events I have held have ranged from taking people to the Open Championship, Wimbledon, Formula 1. But equally impressive have been lower-level motorsports where they got to meet the drivers, a simple lunch/dinner, lake fishing, tickets to a local event, and even an evening axe-throwing!

If your socializing bar is set high, then when it comes to a new sales opportunity where do you go from there? Is the customer now on the hook expecting to buy something? Have you made it too difficult for them to say "no"?

If your competitors are in a race to win the client through their social activities that does not mean you have to join the race. Build a rapport but impress them with your knowledge and skills, your ability to understand and help, not the size of your expense budget.

For any successful business-to-business (B2B) relationship, you do need to socialize. Clients buy from people they like but they buy more from people they trust. Building trust can be done in many ways and having a good rapport. In Neil Strauss' book, *The Game and Rules of the Game*, he states: "Rapport equals Trust plus Comfort."

If there is an emergency, a failure, or an opportunity then you will need the trust of your customer. Build a rapport and you can earn the trust.

Having taken care of the individuals we need also to manage the relationship with the business. Okay, so you cannot take the entire company out for dinner if it is a large corporation and even if it is a small business would you necessarily want to?

Keeping everyone informed of what you do. Keeping everyone aware of your solutions, your successes, and the fact you are keen to continue working with them.

The final piece of the customer relationship is related purely to the individual and their career. It's no different in any team sport. You must know the opposition players, and the roles they play on the field. If they came from another team, find out how they played there and what position they undertook. If they get transferred out, find where they go and compare the departing player with the new arrival. Do this and, when a contact leaves a company, it potentially opens up two opportunities.

If you never got on that well with a key contact perhaps their replacement will fare you better. If you did get on exceptionally well their replacement may become a threat, or worse. If they want to mark their arrival, what better way than to make significant changes—and that means you and your company's products or services.

You may have your work cut out building and growing the new relationship. Start early with any replacement and build on past successes and the history you have had with the company. If they want to make changes, what better way than to give you more business at the cost to your competitors, rather than the other way around. That depth of relationship in the department and the width across the business will help you in achieving this.

In addition, a new opportunity now opens. Follow your previous contact to his or her new company. The company may be different, the role, geography, and their products and services too may all change but keeping in touch may deliver rewards and perhaps not this time but perhaps on the next move.

If you never got on that well with your contact do not assume it will be the same this time. Try to reconnect and re-engage now that the change has been made. Ask them for some honest feedback, it may be the best thing you do and now you are no longer a supplier you might get a lot more information that you did before.

New customers require products or services to be sold to them. Existing accounts typically require more situational selling rather than product selling. Less presentations, more discussions; less need-now, more need-next. Working with clients through this journey will help develop a good sales approach to begin with and one that is sustainable thereafter.

The sales is a continuous pursuit but changes over time. A triathlon is one race, but it requires only one skill at a time and in a set sequence. Throughout the sales pursuit different skills are needed and different personalists to match that of the client. A salesperson plays many roles within the target organization and may have to adopt different personas. Good salespeople know how to navigate a complex organization, know how to manage people, keep a balance between their employer needs and the clients' needs.

Some salespeople are very good at wearing all the hats required of them but fail to close and win business, the most fundamental requirement of a salesperson. That does not make them a bad salesperson, they perhaps have all the skills bar one and investing in personal development could make them a great salesperson. Judging a salesperson on results is a good assessment of the outcomes but if, in doing so, they leave a trail of mess to be cleared up after the results may not justify the means.

When assessing the performance of a salesperson, careful attention should be given to the complete set of skills required, different for account management or for new business sales. Understanding the weak areas and working with them to improve can take an average salesperson from good to great.

I have worked with some exceptional salespeople. I have worked with some that are very capable. I have worked with many that have great talents in many areas but lack one or two key ingredients to be great salespeople. Often the challenge with salespeople is not their ability, rather it is the ability of management to understand the complexity of the role and invest in those areas that need development.

Opportunity Management

We have, to some degree, already covered off the starting point for developing leads from existing customers. Nurturing that relationship so it becomes easy to ask for the sale will help but there is still a lot that must be done in managing a new opportunity.

A lead is a potential new sale in its absolute infancy. A lead often requires patience and some care and attention. Anyone who has tended a garden will know exactly how to manage leads and how to turn leads into prospects.

In a garden, sowing seeds begins long before the start of summer. It is hard work and there is little to show for it when all the hard work is being done. Let us call that "marketing." Any good gardener, whether growing prize-winning pumpkins or simply a nice place to spend time with the family spends time making sure the plants get just the right amount of nutrition and water. Too much and they can die or grow too tall too quickly.

Keeping away the weeds and pests, stopping the crop from being spoiled. Pulling out the weedier looking plants and giving others room to grow, to focus on those that will offer the best and brightest blooms for the longest time.

Lead Management is about putting the groundwork in to identify the best likely prospects for future growth. At the start you may not know if your product is a good fit for their needs. However, you should not pursue all leads and those that you do pursue, not all with the same vigor.

Identifying the right leads will reduce the number of fruitless pursuits but do not be too choosy early on. Taking a narrow view may lose new business that you never suspected and will prevent new ideas from being tried and new products being sold. There is a fine line to follow, and it is never going to be perfect. Some salespeople are hungry for deals that are unrealistic and others not so keen to move out of theirs, and the company's comfort zone.

Qualification is a simple process, and many tools exist to help with this. Done well it will deliver a sharper focus and, like any skill it requires learning and practice to get the best results. Tools such as MEDDICC, BANT, SCOTSMAN—and many more besides—all help the qualification of an opportunity. Qualification is not just done just at the start but should be a regular review point to keep on track and to ensure we focus our efforts continually where we will get the most reward.

Note: MEDDICC = Metrics, Economic Buyer, Decision criteria, Decision process, Identify pain, Champion, Competition. BANT = Budget, Authority, Need, Time. SCOTSMAN = Solution, Competition, Originality, Timescale, Size, Money, Authority, Need.

Once a potential lead is identified then it is about how to reach them. Contacting a person who does not know you and a company that does not use you is called prospecting and includes cold calling—two words that, for some bizarre reason, can strike fear into some of the most hardened of salespeople.

Remember, if you are having a hard time to reach your new client then, aside from the incumbent(s), if there is, everyone else is also having a tough time getting through too.

Marketing

More books have been written on marketing than any other single element of how a company operates. In a simple test in autumn 2021, the word "marketing" returned over 90,000 results in the books section of *Amazon* alone!

Collins Dictionary describes marketing as: ... *the organization of the sale of a product, for example, deciding on its price, the areas it should be supplied to, and how it should be advertised.*

In fact, it is much more than that. Marketing Insider Group explains some of the key elements of marketing as:

- At a fundamental level, marketing is the process of understanding your customers, and building and maintaining relationships with them.
- Marketing is the key to an organization's success, regardless of its size.
- There are several types and subtypes of marketing, digital and offline. You should determine and pursue the ones that work best for you.
- Marketing and Sales teams need to have a unified approach. Automation helps them work toward the same goals.

There are different elements to marketing and different types. Potentially, all of these play a part in different phases of the sales cycle

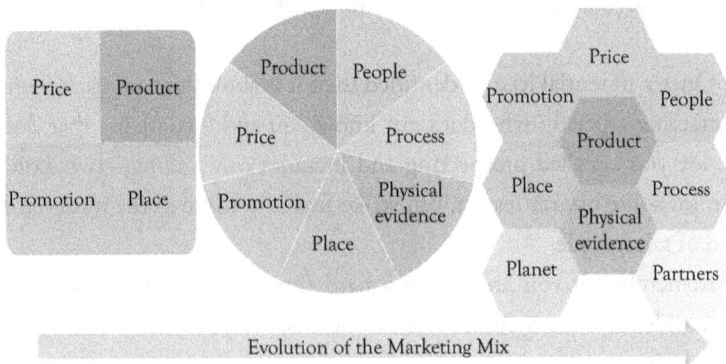

Figure 1.1 *Evolution of the Marketing Mix*

and the pursuit of a customer or opportunity. We often hear reference to "The Marketing Mix." In the 1940s, this consisted of the "4 Ps"—Price, Product, Promotion, and Place. By the 1980s, the general view was this was not enough, and so it was expanded and what became the "7 Ps" now added People, Process, and Physical Evidence. Today I would argue that is no longer sufficient. We need to also consider Planet and Partnerships— The 9 Ps. As shown in Figure 1.1.

How to use marketing, when to deploy different marketing tools, and against which individuals, are a key part of the sales process. Some people are more responsive to the emotional sale and some far more analytical. Similarly, some companies prefer to take a very structured approach to the solutions they buy, and others look for trusted partnerships over the hard facts of it all. Understanding which path to follow is about understanding the customer and employing the tools and the tactics needed to win them over.

Add to this the complexity of cultural and social norms and what works for one company may not apply in another. In Japan, there is a long history of crossholding of shares between companies up and down the supply chain, known as *Keiretsu*. From the west, this "cozy relationship" seems odd as it gets in the way sometimes of competitive tendering and a drive for cost savings and efficiency. In troubled times, companies can resemble a stack of cards or dominos more than a cohesive foundation. *Keiretsu* may increase or decrease the chance of winning business and may block outsiders and innovation as well as financial competitiveness. So much so that the Japanese Prime Minister, Shinzo Abe, (2006–2007 and 2012–2014) put into place new codes of corporate governance to try and unwind these structures. Today some companies have progressed well, but others remain stubborn to the old ways.

Sales!

"Sales" is a part of the sales process and, judging by the wording, a fundamental part. But sales can be won and lost long before we get to the actual "rubber meets the road" section and can also be lost even after the ink has dried. The losing team or referee may not call for a video replay but failure to perform and cooling off periods give a corporate client much

Figure 1.2 Keywords for "Sales"

Figure 1.3 Keywords for the sales process

more leeway that a sports team. Taking what matters for sales and putting it into a word cloud based on a research for this book, as shown in Figure 1.2.

Take away the words *sales* and *salesperson* and the critical words for sales take on a somewhat different perspective, as shown in "Figure 1.3."

We can see from the second word cloud, sales clearly have several fundamental elements: process, the market, the company, winning (of course), the need, time (commitment), and doing more—more than the competition, more than the customer expects, more effort, more commitment.

Sales is the pursuit of an opportunity to an outcome. Hopefully, a successful outcome, but if not then it is an opportunity to learn. Think of it this way, if you lose a deal, you have just joined the *Winback team*! Although being part of the *Winback Creation Team* may not be something to be so proud about.

Sales as a pursuit has, as we have already stated, a clear objective: to win the deal. It also has several resources required—personnel, material, products, and systems—and clear steps along the way, some of which may encourage you to continue, and some may tell you it is time to quit. Remember, in any competitive bid situation there are two winners: those who win the deal and those who decided not to pursue it early and saved time and money, which they used on deals they could win.

Sales requires you to be able to engage with customers, provide them information, respond to questions, delight, and excite. But it also requires you to chase the customer, perhaps even if they do not want to be, to handle objections and to overcome obstacles. Sales can be a "Tough Mudder" more than a 100-meter sprint, you may come away bruised and beaten and with no medal. But, for anyone that has run a marathon, just crossing the line is exhilarating, and makes you want more. Winning takes it to a whole new level and knowing how to win requires training.

Implementation

When you win the deal, it is often tempting just to throw it over the office wall at the delivery team. After all, you have done your job, now it is their turn. That would be a mistake.

Salespeople rarely make good project managers. Myself, having completed a PRINCE2 (PRojects IN Controlled Environments, version 2) Project Management qualification, I can see why. That is not to say some people cannot transition from Sales to PM and back, but it is a rare breed that can do this well.

As a salesperson you are not expected to hold the hand of the Project Manager, or indeed the customer, through implementation. But making sure the baton is passed efficiently from-sold-to-start can make a difference. More importantly is not to overpromise and under-deliver, or worse, promise things that cannot be delivered.

Far too many times have salespeople commit to the undeliverable or, to keep a customer happy, promise things now that are not yet on the roadmap or perhaps are but not due any time soon.

I was working for a company and inherited a problem from a now departed salesperson. The salesman sold a huge data solution to the customer and one that could not be delivered. The team tried in vain to deliver on what had been promised and kept failing. The customer became increasingly frustrated. So much so the client implemented an internal audit and found an altogether different solution that would save them in excess of £1 million and have no need for the solution already sold.

I was called in because the customer had not paid their, very significant, bill. Indeed, it should have been paid before the start of the project but for almost twelve months they had been dragging their heels whilst we tried to satisfy the sale. The situation was that my employer wanted paying, and the customer now wanted out of the contract.

I recall walking into my first meeting with this well-known international corporation to be met by the Information Technology Director, Finance Director and Head of Procurement. So much for an introductory meeting! It did not go well.

It matters not what the outcome was, we lost and agreed to cancel the bill and cancel the project. The salesperson had already been paid and had left the company. I was quite happy that we did the right thing, my Finance Director was not as impressed!

Why the Sales Manager felt it okay to sign off on the deal I never fully understood, but he left very shortly after we resolved the matter with the client.

This is a great example of a salesperson overselling and focusing on the sales (and commission) rather than the bigger objective of winning good, repeatable business and growing the customer relationship to ever greater opportunities.

The true outcome was far more than the £1 million that we eventually wrote off. Less than a year later this international company decided to outsource its entire global data network. Once again, I was called in to try and make sure we put the past behind us, and the salesperson was not damaged by his predecessor.

Over a nice lunch in a quiet restaurant the IT Director told me it would be better if we do not bid. Whilst he liked what we had done and was very appreciative of my involvement, the damage had been done. There was no way we would be allowed to win any more business with them.

That £1 million we wrote off, that was but a small percentage of the opportunity lost. The salesperson kept his commission and the Sales Manager also, but the company they both worked for at the time lost out considerably.

Having won a piece of business, a good salesperson should attend the project kick-off meeting. It shows commitment to the customer and builds rapport with the wider team. The salesperson, despite not being overall in charge of delivery, should always make sure they are accessible to the customer and to the delivery team in case they want to discuss progress or obstacles.

Support

Once a project has been implemented, notwithstanding upgrades or later changes, then it falls to the business to support the customer and the solution. At this point, any salesperson might be forgiven for thinking it is no longer their responsibility. "Forgiven" because yes, for the greatest part, it is not a salesperson's responsibility. But, in much the same way salespeople should not oversell the product they should also not overpromise on support.

Some companies are structured with separate Sales and Account Management. Some people prefer to hunt, others go fishing. Smaller companies may not be organized this way and salespeople carry a sales target and some accounts, so they are responsible for selling and retaining.

It is important an Account Manager has a handle on the ongoing operations of an account and, while they do not need to know the details of every minor glitch, knowing about big issues or being abreast of ongoing causes of concern is important.

A large international bank was using a system a predecessor had sold to them. Over the years the account had little attention and was a guaranteed source of income, placing little demand on us as a supplier. Because of the nature of their business and what we offered there was very little upsell or cross-sell opportunity.

I heard a rumour a competitor, with a much broader offering, was starting to talk to our client. When I asked the Sales Manager, it was made clear that the account was unmanaged and, therefore, was now my account.

When your first meeting with a client is the first time anyone has been to see them in over a year and when they are talking to a competitor it is always going to be a challenging meeting.

The situation was made worse by the recent audit that found the client had upgraded their hardware and, as the licence was based on the performance of the hardware in MIPS (millions of instructions per second) it meant they owed us some more licence revenue.

As a salesperson I had a choice. Go for the licence upgrade, start a legal argument, and then lose the entire business to the competitor. Or review the agreement, make amendments and have them commit for a longer term. I chose the latter and we eventually won an extension to the contract by changing the terms and saw an existing revenue stream extended but not grow.

Had the account been properly managed we could have come to the negotiating table earlier and found a mid-path between the price for the hardware upgrade impact and the current and extended the contract. A lack of attention to an existing account cost us in the long term. Had I not been made aware of the competitor threat we could have lost it completely.

Being aware of the ongoing situation is not just for Account Managers and is not just for your products and services. Salespeople need to be aware of what is on their customer's plate, not just what is on their own. Walking into a meeting when all is well in your world, does not mean all is well in theirs. Your competitors, as well as those you do not compete against, may tip the balance for you or against you depending on how prepared you are.

Being up to date is easy with modern technology. Access to news feeds and using tools to make sure you get the news that is relevant to your prospective customer is easy. Done well it can be a positive advantage, showing you have an interest in your target and are perceived to have a wider knowledge of them, their competitors, their customers, and their market.

The Process

Selling is a project. But it operates within an ongoing cycle of events. This cycle of events will sometimes work for you and sometimes against you, but always it will have an impact. The process also involves not just you and your organization but that of the prospective new customer, or existing customer.

Taking sales as an isolated pursuit is a focused way of winning new business. But, as an isolated pursuit, one needs to be aware of the world outside this very project that is a sales opportunity. Winning one deal is like winning a match, but you need to win more than one for a successful season. As with sport, winning is also infectious, it impacts the people around you, your competition gets to hear about it and will change their tactics accordingly, potential clients will start to notice you as well. How often we see teams defeated before they get on the pitch.

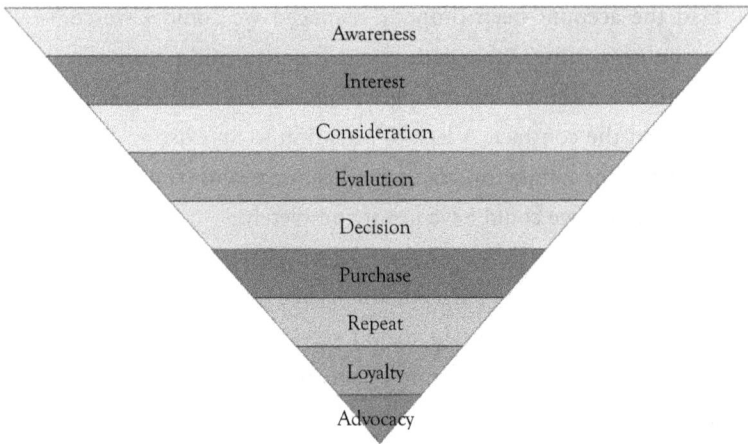

Figure 1.4 The Sales Funnel

Sales may be a clearly defined process, but it sits among a fog of information and disinformation, good data and missing data, good and bad intentions, skilled people, and those less capable, and not forgetting the buyers' own processes, which may be altogether different to yours!

Despite all this in every sale, there is a journey that you and the customer will go through. It applies to anything from buying a quick lunch from a take-away diner to a holiday, or life insurance, or even applying for a job.

The four elements of the sale are simply Awareness, Interest, Consideration, and Purchase. It really is that simple. Making it happen how you want, however, can be a whole lot more complex!

The Sales Funnel—see Figure 1.4 above—or Marketing Funnel or Conversion Funnel was developed by advertising specialist Elias St. Elmo Lewis in 1898. It was originally called as the Purchase Funnel. However, it did not really come to prominence until 1924 and a publication by William Townsend, a lecturer at Columbia University and later referenced by Edward K. Strong Jr. in *The Psychology of Selling and Advertising*. Over the years, some of the letters have been changed by various interpreters but the principles remain.

The Sales Funnel starts wide and not overly focused at the start—although there certainly needs a little focus—and narrows down as it progresses, spilling out unwanted customers and opportunities as it progresses.

Today, the Sales/Marketing Funnel has been tuned and developed and has many variations, each adopted by different training companies and users alike. However, it all follows the same basic method, albeit with some additional steps and narrowing of the funnel.

The objective of **Awareness** is to introduce your brand or product/service to potential customers. In this book, we are focused more on how to reach potential customers through marketing campaigns. But Awareness can be created through advertising (online and physical), improved Search Engine Optimization (SEO), social media, events, campaigns, or in the case of existing customers targeted cross-sell development and referrals.

Being aware of you/your product is not enough. Salespeople must make potential customers interested in what they are selling. Building a relationship with potential new customers starts here. Brand values, company values, and basic product information are the focus at this stage. This is not about selling at this stage. Good content matters the most here.

Awareness today can be achieved in many ways but, perhaps the most obvious ways to get your potential future customer aware of your product is:

- Whitepaper
- Product guide/e-Guide
- Buyer checklist
- Educational videos
- Article (thought leadership)
- Blog/Vlog
- Advertising (online or physical)

For the potential customer, merely knowing who the supplier is and having qualified them as a potential supplier is not enough to buy. The fact the buyer may like the product and does not disagree with the company's values is not going to make the products fly off the shelf. For the vast majority of buying decisions, we all weigh up the pros and cons of multiple suppliers or products. Whether that is buying a bar of chocolate in a shop or investing in a new savings bond it is all about evaluating (next step) but before that any buyer needs to shortlist based on some simple assessment. That is unless the buyer wants to waste a huge amount of time evaluating every supplier.

Consideration can be left with the customer to decide but sales and marketing can help them make the "right decision" too:

- Free webinars
- Case studies
- References
- Free samples
- Specification sheets
- Product catalogs
- Advertising/Infomercials
- Customer advocacy and referral campaigns

After the first sift of Consideration, customers **Evaluate** multiple potential suppliers. It matters here that the customer finds it easy to navigate the information that will sway their decision positively in your favor (and hide the stuff that you do not want them to know).

Not every customer has the same needs/wants/desires and not every customer goes through the same process of evaluation, or indeed has the same values. Companies cannot serve all their potential customers equally and even the ones they already have you cannot serve equally too. Understanding the most likely items of Consideration, the most impactful and the ones that differentiate you from the competition, need to be brought to the fore.

Companies may want to offer a free trial as part of the Consideration phase. This perhaps works for some products better than others, a weekend test drive of a car, someone standing with a plate and "try me" at a food convention/market, open day for a club or group, samples and giveaways received in the post.

After all this, we might get a buying **Decision**. Decisions are not binary: yes or no. The customer could buy multiples, they could buy from multiple suppliers, or they could defer/delay their decision. In which case they revert to the Interest/Consideration layer of the funnel to begin the process another day.

In the world of business sales, there are often multiple decision makers, plus influencers, evaluators, blockers, and other roles that play out throughout the sales pursuit. Something as simple as buying a young child's new bicycle engages the user and the buyer (child and parents). In this example, the sales agent would tailor their sales message and comments equally to both parties to win the heart of the child and mind of the ultimate decision maker. The same messages would be applied in different ways and different messages may be put discretely to the parent or the child to win the deal.

Deciding to buy is not the same as buying. In the example above, the child may have made the decision but, unless independently wealthy enough at this stage, is unlikely to proceed and even then, the shop may have issue with a six-year-old handing over a wad of cash.

In business, there is often a separation between buyer and decision maker. A new coffee machine may be purchased on expenses for the office chat room, but a new call handling system may be evaluated by the IT Department, the Call Center Manager, and perhaps even some of the team, but it may well be Procurement or the office of the Chief Finance Officer that makes the final decision and places the order.

Even when a customer has made the decision to buy, they may not **Purchase**. Shopping online and deciding what you want could then lead you on a search for alternative suppliers. Similarly, visiting the shops to find what you want may then move you to online to make the purchase. Even things as simple as shops not accepting cash for small purchase items. Or the fact the coffee shop will only provide a plastic cup rather than one of recycled material or a reusable crockery. There are multiple reasons why a Decision made is not a Purchase. Just because the customer has made the decision does not mean they will go through with it. Make the sale as easy as possible, pain-free, and positively enjoyable.

It was *Nissan* in 2014 that coined the phrase: *"Eat, Sleep, Race, Repeat."* Versions of that should be posted on every wall of every sales office, marketing department, and customer call center. Repeat business is the lowest cost and, ultimately, most loyal business.

The majority of Sales/Marketing Funnels stop at Purchase and perhaps this is where the funnel truly ends and a new one begins for repeat business. The problem with that is once you reach the bottom of the funnel, everyone forgets about the next funnel, so it makes more sense to keep it as one and have included Repeat at the base of the funnel.

How you turn a one-time-purchase customer into a loyal customer is down to several things; good initial purchase, similar values, CRM system, product development, further value-add products or services, a good product, and customer relationship (people not the system).

Customer loyalty is a subject for which many books have been written. According to Customer Insight Group: *"Customer loyalty can be defined as a customer's faithfulness and commitment to a business. The measure of loyalty is often based on consumer preferences, the degree of satisfaction, the frequency of purchase, fidelity, price sensitivity, and brand advocacy."*

Once you have established **Customer Loyalty**, customers develop a preference for your brand or company, more than they do a specific product. *Apple* is perhaps the best example of brand loyalty today. Their brand of smartphone has allowed them to push up prices, develop new products with the same look and feel, and drive down the upgrade cycle time. They have developed new products and continued to expand their range. In mid-2021, Apple reported quarterly revenue of $81.4 billion.

Loyalty does not make repeat purchases more likely because you remind them of it, but because they genuinely like your product. Customer loyalty is, therefore, not just repeat purchase. Customers need to see the relationship between their supplier and themselves as more than a transactional relationship. Loyalty does also not just happen by chance after the sale and repeat sale. Loyalty requires a strong relationship management, shared values, and perhaps even a loyalty program.

Beyond Loyalty exists **Advocacy**. This occurs when your loyal customers become fans. *Apple* for example has a lot of fans. Queuing up for hours on end the night before a new phone launch just to get their hands on the next version of a smartphone, or other product. Advocates will try and convince others to buy the product, typically rejecting any negative press or trying to qualify it to their peer group and often blind to alternatives or some of the details they would rather not know.

The Sales/Marketing Funnel leads to an outcome: it does not take the sales project ("the sale") and feed back into the sales process. The continuation of the process requires repeat purchases, loyalty, and then advocacy.

These last three are what stimulates demand for the next funnel, and so it continues.

Remember, selling is about winning but, as comedian Groucho Marx said *"If you're not having fun, you're probably doing something wrong."*

Key Takeaways

Every organization whether profitable or not needs to focus on the sale and win new business. Even not-for-profit organizations must maintain a steady flow of new interest and generate new business. To do this effectively requires the will of the people working in the organization working as a team on the task at hand. That task being to retain and grow existing clients and to secure new, profitable clients.

The easiest sales are to existing customers. The cost to retain a customer is significantly lower than the cost of acquiring a new one. Many studies exist to work out what the ratio is of cost to retain and cost to win but for every industry and every geography the cost is different. However, it is universally accepted that retaining is always far less expensive to retain existing than to win new.

Understanding how to secure long-term retention and lock-in clients is a key place to start for business survival. Identifying what new products and services to sell them can only work if indeed you have something new to sell them. But as we have seen in this chapter, that requires commitment, and it requires finding the right balance in the relationship you have with the client. It does not always go to plan but having the tools and the team to manage it can make all the difference. In all matters relating to existing clients, the relationship is key.

Understanding what a genuine opportunity is and what has a realistic chance of success will reduce wasted effort and lost time. Tools exist to qualify and to keep requalifying opportunities to ensure salespeople and the wider sales team remain on track to success. We mentioned BANT, MEDDICC, and SCOTSMAN and these are certainly tools worth checking out in more detail, along with ANUM, CHAMP, FAINT, and NEAT—there are others. Choosing one that works for you and for your industry, your company, product, and service will increase the likelihood of success. Being consistent in how it is applied and reapplied by different members of the team ensures the company focuses where it matters to win most often.

Wrapping around the sale is the oft-neglected partner of the sales pursuit: marketing. Knowing the relative values of the 9 Ps (Chapter 4) and how they relate to each market, each product, and each customer is important but using all the tools as levers is critical in the success of the marketing team to elevate the sales opportunity to greater chance of success.

The Sales Funnel provides structure to the wider sales process and helps identify progress as well as giving check gates to allow decisions on whether to continue pursuit. We mentioned a range of tools that can be used from White Papers to Webinars, from Product Sheets to Testimonials. All of these, and more, combine to form the Content Marketing Matrix, covered later.

Identifying the right marketing approach and using the right marketing tools provides a foundation for sales. To really do the subject of marketing justice in understanding how to win at sales would significantly add to the volume of this book, it simply cannot be understated. However, while marketing and sales may be "joined at the hip," they too remain separate subjects altogether.

As we have seen. After the sale is won, it requires the salesperson to keep the win. Implementation is, of course, a key to success and it needs to be handled correctly and with the salesperson involved. It begins even before that with selling a product or service the customer wants and one that can be delivered. A salesperson focusing purely on the commission check is not only bad for business right now but bad for future potential business.

And when the deal is won, every day you must make sure that you keep winning. Adding value when you can, keeping competitors at bay, retaining the trust of the client, and securing long-term future success. Account Management is critical in long-term consistent revenue. It may lack the sharp edge of new business sales and, in many organizations, does not have the same importance, but it should. A well-managed account costs less and often delivers more than a new piece of business.

When all the component parts are aligned: marketing, new business sales, product delivery, account management, customer retention, customer satisfaction, and support, it can deliver huge financial benefits and growth opportunities to any company. But to do this effectively it needs a process, a game plan. It needs each of the players to know what part they play in moving the ball around the field of play, what it takes to score and what is needed to defend.

The Sales Funnel is a simple model and easy for any company to adopt. It can be adjusted to suit each company or products and tweaked to suit the needs of each pursuit. It provides a logical evaluation, a simple process, and a path toward the final objective.

Without a process, without a plan, and without the right team of players committed to win, there is no season success. Perhaps the occasional win and very often some heavy defeats. To keep winning, everyone needs to understand the part they play and the importance that it brings to the team's success. Not everyone has a chance to run out onto the field of play, some are in the dugouts and some back at base looking at data or preparing the fuel the team needs.

We will look at these key components in more detail through the book.

CHAPTER 2

The Product (Service)

Overview

When a salesperson is asked about their product or service, it is often seen less about truly understanding the product, rather an opportunity to recall and recite product facts. Knowing the load weight of a commercial vehicle or the internal cubic volume of a fridge may be useful to the conversation as pieces of factual content, but they hardly smack of detailed product knowledge when applied to the customer and their needs, when applied to the market and its needs, and when applied to future customers and future markets.

A chapter on the product or service, therefore, is not about the importance of learning by rote facts and figures but is instead about the importance of positioning the product against the competition, knowing where you sit and they sit, know where to go next, where to pursue, and where not to engage.

In this chapter, we will look at the product as it is today and what the potential is for the future. How to understand the market changes that impact on a product and how to react to them, or better still how to make them work in your favor. Simply knowing the product of today and the direction a company wants to take it requires a structured approach. When this direction is taking on a new competitor, it matters to understand how the customer sees your product, not just how the marketing team wants to position it. The largest companies and the smallest businesses are all prone to failure.

In September 2013, *Microsoft* acquired *Nokia*. At the press conference to announce the $7.17 billion takeover *Nokia* then CEO Stephen Elop announced *"We didn't do anything wrong, but somehow, we lost."* What *Nokia* did was simply not to understand the future direction of the market and the needs of the customer and not keep up with future trends and current needs.

International expansion, for any company, is fraught with danger. It can have a dramatic impact on the overall performance of the company and, on occasions, may even bring down a company. Cultural differences in the customer, buying behaviors and even the name all need to be understood. A market entry strategy defined only once the likelihood of success is known and seen as worth the risk. But that does not mean it is a slam dunk, and some great companies have found, to their cost, that a lack of preparation has dramatic consequences.

Knowledge About Your Product
Not Product Knowledge

It might seem obvious that, at some point in the Sales Process, we should consider the product(s) or service(s) we are selling. Knowing what the best products and services are, which of these benefit the company the most and which add little value, financially or otherwise, is not always obvious and, for more than a few companies, something they fail to fully understand.

In 1957, the prototype "Orange Box" was produced and by 1959 went into production as the *BMC Mini*. In its day, a much-loved car. Unbelievably the car stayed in production until 2000. We are talking here about the 3-m long, 1.4-m wide box on wheels, not the modern, *BMW* variant. The car was a reaction to the changing demands because of the then current fuel crisis.

Prior to launch, *BMC* never realized what a huge success the car would go on to be. What makes the story of the Mini interesting is how *Ford* reacted. Aware that *BMC* was working on a new car and having seen it in the flesh some years before it went on sale, *Ford* too were working on upgrading a successful small family saloon and, in 1959 introduced the new Ford Anglia.

The *Anglia* had an oddly designed rear-raked rear screen and came pretty spartan, no glove box door, or passenger sun-visor; even the heater was extra. In bringing this to market, *Ford* realized they had a fight on their hands and so the price was a very keen £589 0s 11d—it matters nought if you cannot work out your Pounds, Shillings, and Pence. For every *Anglia* sold *Ford* made a loss.

What *Ford* saw with the *Mini* was a small saloon car trying to take some of their market. As a result, they shaved off some of the product features and set their price at a level that would sell, it was marginally more expensive than the *Mini*.

We can accept that in the 1950s the technology did not exist and the attention to detail on the supply chain did not allow them the level of cost detail we would expect today. However, instead of making the *Anglia* a higher value product, adding in heating, and so on (later they added a rear wiper at no cost!) and setting the price accordingly *Ford* decided to go against a car that, today, few people would agree they were direct market competitors.

Knowing your product or service, its value to your clients, the position you sit in the marketplace and the competition you are truly up against is key to any sale.

I was working for a client, a successful business, growing and profitable. However, despite several reviews and changes they had not achieved the profitability they felt they deserved. The company was, in all other respects, a great company.

The investigation we undertook pared every cost right back and broke apart the entire sales process. Every won deal and lost deal was measured, and costs applied. For fixed costs, these were even split differently based on the complexity of contracting or different regional requirements, even down to the time to draft special clauses. A weighty piece of analysis but with good reason.

The final report demonstrated that one sector they felt was successful, did indeed bring in a good level of income. But, because of the additional requirements, the more complex sales cycle and even local culture, the margin was considerably less than most other sales. Had this been a small part of their business the impact would have been less. Because it accounted for a significant part of their business, they were generating revenues that did little to add profit to the business.

To address this, my client simply changed their approach to this market. They played hard with new clients in the sector. They chased less deals and won less deals but the deals they won cost less to serve and had better margin. The time saved enabled them to focus on other sectors and even develop two new product offerings to another market.

The financial results showed a significant uplift and, with new products coming onstream the company ramped up its recruitment so they could sell even more of the good stuff.

It is important to understand what is really adding to the performance of the company and what is a successful sale that adds little incremental value. Being successful is not about winning more deals, it is about winning more of the right kind of deals.

Understanding the products and services you sell is not about reading the fact sheets or knowing what the Unique Selling Points (USPs) are. It encompasses the market fit, the competition, what is the best use of resources, be that financial or human resource.

Being able to identify the best product to lead with, it may even be loss-making. Knowing what the best cross-sell or upsell is, for the supplier and for the customer. Recognizing that not all products should be sold in all markets and that pricing may vary from one to another—and how to manage that when a client points it out.

Knowing when to launch a product, and when to pull one is also a part of understanding your product strategy. Knowing what product comes next in the sale to an existing client; and knowing when to enter new markets and which product to lead with. All these are elements required to understand your product. Knowing your product is not about what you sell today to whom, but what you can sell tomorrow as well and to whom else.

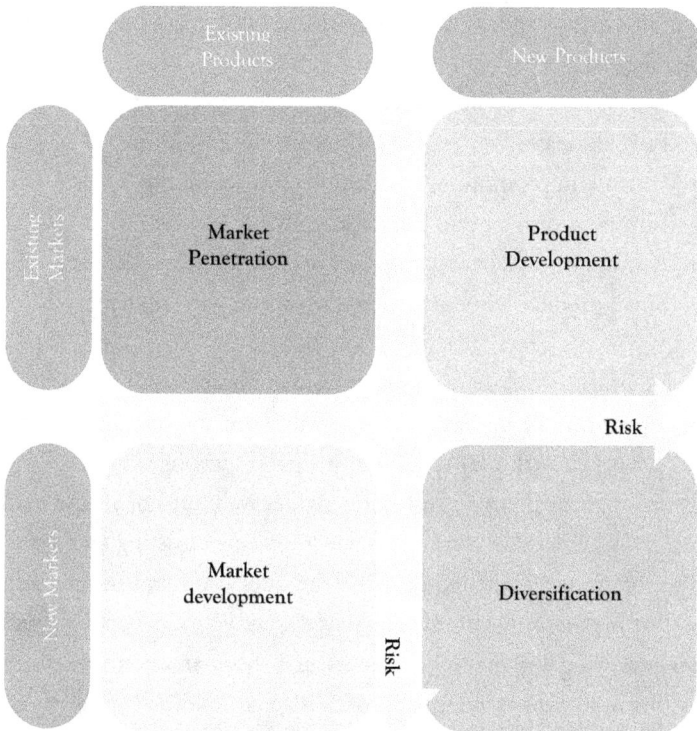

Figure 2.1 The Ansoff Matrix (Ansoff 1957)

In 1957, Russian-born, now U.S. citizen Igor Ansoff's article in the *Harvard Business Review* entitled *"Strategies for Diversification"* developed what we now know as the Ansoff Matrix (see above, Figure 2.1). It focused on four areas: market penetration, market development, product development, and diversification.

Existing Products in Existing Markets

Developing your existing market from your existing product range is the lowest risk and, very often, least rewarding way to grow a business. This is less about product development more about market share and, sometimes, a greater market share does not mean greater profits and rarely means improved profit margins.

Sales is simply about selling more stuff. It does not have to be the same stuff or indeed to the same people. But to sell more stuff, you need to find new buyers and, in an existing market that requires one, or more, of the following:

- Price decrease
- Increase in promotion, advertising, and marketing
- Improved distribution capabilities/ability to serve
- Acquisition of a product/service rival in the same market
- Small product refinements/enhancements/development

Some of these will deliver greater results; numbers of units sold, revenues, or profits. To understand what will work the best and what will deliver what you wish may require some market testing.

It may well be that you serve one market well but not all the market segments. Whether that constitutes new markets or existing markets is an opinion often hotly debated between the sales team and the marketing team. But making sure you have achieved what you can from the market means reviewing the market segments first. Segmentation can come in many forms, but the standard approaches are as follows:

- Geographic
- Cultural
- Sociodemographic
- Behavioral

We should step away from the Ansoff Matrix at this point and look at the *Boston Consulting Group* (BCG) Matrix, Figure 2.2.

Occasionally referred to as the Growth-Share Matrix, it was developed by BCG Founder Bruce Henderson in 1968 to help companies focus their production lines and marketing on their most profitable products. As a tool the BCG Matrix is quite a blunt instrument and, for that reason, better serves when working with other tools.

The BCG Matrix considers only the current market and current products. Accepted that is its purpose but, it does so without consideration for cashflow, limits of production capacity or scarce resources, supply chain limits, and total demand for products or services.

BCG lacks an understanding of seasonality and of short-term spikes in demand. A Cash Cow may seem a good thing for income but there

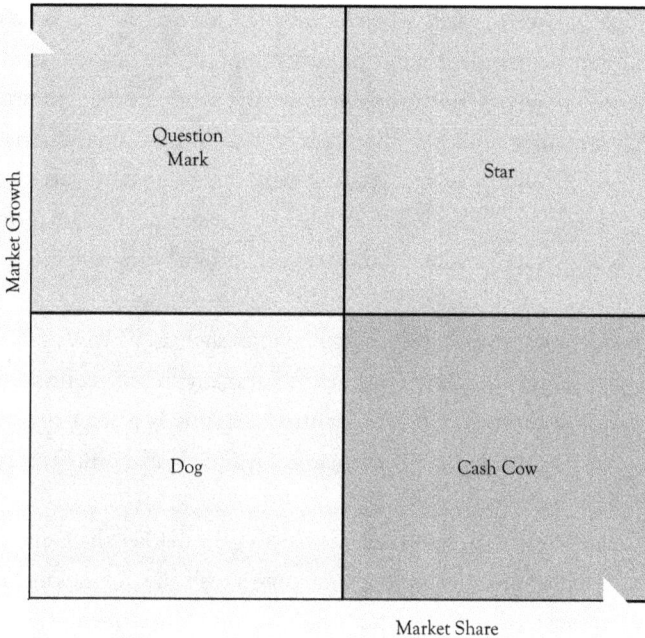

Figure 2.2 The BCG Matrix

could be other products developed that, over time, become more profitable but do not get the resource needed because the focus is on serving the current cash generator.

Cash Cows are there to be "milked" as they are, they are not really going anywhere unless others are willing to invest in winning business in a static market. Income generated from Cash Cows gives companies the opportunity to invest in new products or new markets for further growth. Despite the term "cash" net margin makes better sense than income. Generally, Cash Cows should not gain significant additional investment other than to keep them current or to maintain market share.

Where a company has a low market share compared to competitors and operates in a slowly growing market it can be a **Dog**. While general thinking is that they are not worth investing in, a view of potential future market growth should always be taken, not just current market position. What is a Dog today may become A Question-Mark tomorrow. For Dogs, it is always important to perform deeper analysis of each market to make sure they are not worth investing in for future potential.

High growth markets where companies have a low market share are something that requires better understanding of the future potential and whether to pursue. **Question-Marks** are the products that require closest attention as they could be the Stars of the future. Often referred to as a Problem Child, these markets can very often consume large amounts of investment incurring losses, at least in the short, or short-to-medium term. Not every Question-Mark pays off and knowing when to quit is a difficult decision to make.

In recent years, we have seen companies such as *WeWork, Uber, Snap, AirBnB, Deliveroo, Pinterest, Slack, and* many more, continually lose eye-watering sums of money. For investors this is a long play and for many will one day hopefully turn a profit. Question-Marks and Problem Child have never been more apt.

A Question-Mark has the potential to gain market share and become a star, which would later, perhaps, become a cash cow. Question-Marks do not always succeed and even after large amount of investments they struggle to gain market share and eventually become dogs. Therefore, they require very close consideration to decide if they are worth investing in or not.

Stars, as well as generating good income they also demand investment to maintain share and profits. It is important here to understand two things for a Star market. The cost required to maintain market share and the investment required to grow market share. Some star markets can be extremely demanding financially.

In rapidly changing industries, where innovation is key to stay at the forefront and where new products and technology can quickly change the market it is vital to keep investing. Investment can be in research and/or development (R&D), marketing, acquisition of competitors or suppliers, and changes to your market approach. To remain a Star, it can require consistent and significant investment as a result.

The BCG Matrix has been used as a basis for other models. Originally called the General Electric Multifactorial Analysis, later the GE-McKinsey Matrix (Figure 2.3), offers a slightly more complex view of product or service strength set against attractiveness to invest in a market. It follows many of the same principles but is more nuanced and gives a more detailed assessment of options.

Both these matrixes are a place to start rather than a final assessment of what course to follow. A decision on the course of action should be based on detailed analysis of the market today and future potential, the demand and what is required for future product development. It should also be something reviewed periodically to understand what has changed and the impact thereof.

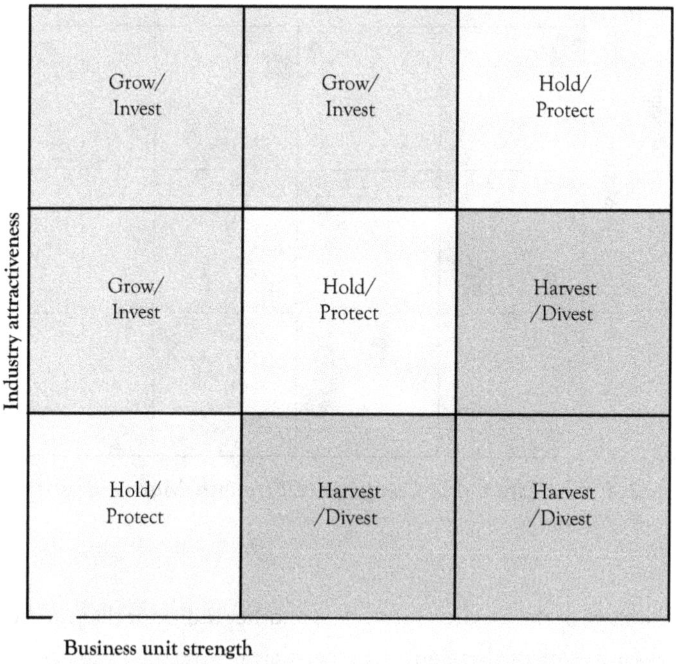

Grow/Invest	Grow/Invest	Hold/Protect
Grow/Invest	Hold/Protect	Harvest/Divest
Hold/Protect	Harvest/Divest	Harvest/Divest

Industry attractiveness

Business unit strength

Figure 2.3 The GE-McKinsey matrix

Taking a forward-looking view, the Life Cycle-Competitive Strength Matrix (see Figure 2.4) analyses the competitive strength of your product offering against the maturity of the product itself. Almost all products have a life cycle, whether it is the latest technology, restaurants, cars, even houses. True the house may still be standing when we sell it but as life changes and family demands change the individual demand for that specific product changes. Few items have a never-ending life cycle, typically this would only be staple foods such as bread, rice, and so on.

Starbucks opened its first store in 1971. It was not until 1988 that it opened its first store outside Seattle. That's a very slow start to what is a huge company today. *Rovio Entertainment Oyj* developed 51 games before it developed *Angry Birds*.

Stage of market life cycle

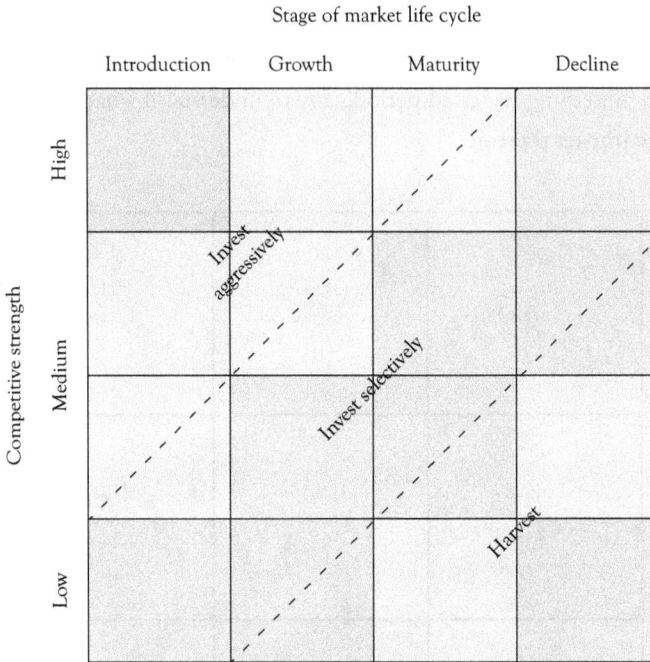

Figure 2.4 The Life Cycle-Competitive Strength Matrix

The stage of the product life cycle is another indicator that can be used to make investment decisions, whether that is investment in the market to grow the business or market share or investment in the product to retain or gain new customers.

For most products, the maturity curve is shortening. Typically, a product will go through four stages: Introduction, Growth, Maturity, and Decline. Introduction for start-ups is proving more difficult and the number of failures at this stage is increasing. Once growth is reached very often the need to innovate and develop to maintain at the top becomes more demanding as product life cycles shorten.

Moving away from Existing Products in Existing Markets, we can focus on the other three portions of the Ansoff Matrix.

Market Development

Taking an existing product to a new market may not seem the most high-risk approach to growing your product sales but a lack of local knowledge can cost you dearly as *Starbucks* found out when they launched in Australia. They are not the only big company to get it wrong.

Tesco is a dominant player in the UK supermarket sector with over 7,000 stores worldwide and revenues, in 2019, of £63.9 billion. In 2007, *Tesco* launched into the United States. Timing was bad just before the 2008 financial crisis but, with the deep pockets *Tesco* had, they can afford to weather the storm. Unlike their competitors, *Tesco* did not see the value in coupons and had no loyalty card, well not until their last year of trading in the United States. In hard times, coupons become a required element for the shopper, certainly much more so in the United States than in Europe. Something *Tesco* failed to understand.

The *Tesco, Fresh and Easy* stores were more local than the big super-markets. Suited to European shoppers, but not what the American shop-per is used to and not what the American shopper wants in the main from a supermarket. There are several other errors *Tesco* made, self-checkouts, own-brand, low population density states, and so on.

In 2012, five years after launching, *Tesco* quit the United States. sell-ing 150 of its approximately 200 stores. *Tesco* racked up losses of $1.6 billion for their troubles. Proof that if a company this big and successful can get it wrong, then anyone can. Size is no guarantee of success.

Before entering a new market, research is needed. Research what the customer wants and what the competition offers. Make sure you have a product that will sell and a way to sell it that will appeal. Entering a new market may be low risk but that does not mean it is no risk.

As well as new territories, new markets may include new market seg-ments. Some may argue that it is the same market, but we will come back to that at the end.

CAGE Distance Framework

In 2011, Professor Pankaj Ghemawat, developed the CAGE Distance Framework, made up of Cultural, Administrative, Geographic, and Eco-nomic Distances to be measured Unilaterally, Bilaterally, and Multilater-ally. Figure 2.5, gives a more detailed graphical representation.

To undertake a CAGE Distance, assessment can require a consider-able amount of work and requires much local knowledge. Companies, some quite large, have either failed to do this well or have not used it

Distance			
Cultural	**Administrative**	**Geo-graphic**	**Economic**
Language	Bureaucracy	Size	Models
Religion	Regional models	Nearby countries	Currency
Tradition	National models	Weather	Growth rates
Values	Requirements	Political borders	GDP per capita
Social norms	Politics	Geography /Geology	Productivity

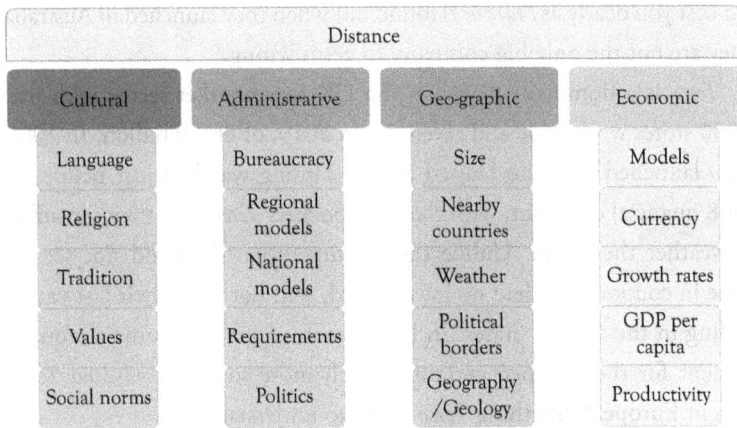

Figure 2.5 CAGE Distance Framework

effectively before embarking on an international expansion. For most of us, however, it may be a useful thing to know perhaps more than something used with definite intent.

Cultural refers to language, beliefs, cultural norms, social hierarchy, and framework, religious, and attitudes toward both domestic and international matters. In the *Tesco* example previously, the cultural requirements of shoppers in the United States and their commitment to vouchers, the location of stores and shopping preferences would, or should, have all been identified had the company conducted a thorough assessment using the CAGE Distance Framework. Despite the fact the UK and United States share a common language and have many cultural similarities that does not guarantee all other cultural alignments remain the same.

Administrative differences consider not just governmental and political but historical norms, such as the past relationship between the two countries, especially relevant in countries with colonial ties. Beyond that it also refers to complexity of trading including currencies, tax, and law.

Of course, **Geographical Distance** is often a part to play in international expansion. However, think not only of distance but also topographical features, climate, border issues, and the ability to serve the new market not just reach it. Consideration should be given to the internal geography and supply chain requirements.

Finally, the **Economic Distance** between the two markets such as the cost of doing business as well as the affordability of your product in the new market.

All of this is set against Bilateral and Unilateral considerations. Consider how the two markets (countries perhaps) compare. How they trade between, and that the relationship is between the two. For Unilateral, how the new market stands not regarding your current market or point of origin.

Anyone who has travelled internationally can readily recall things that had novelty appeal and those that would never work back in their own country. Enjoying a German Bratwurst in many Western countries perhaps has greater appeal than a curried donut from Japan or chickens' feet from China. Similarly, pickled herring has more appeal in Scandinavia and central Europe than the Middle East and south Asia. For companies looking to expand it is not enough to simply have a general understanding it requires a structured approach and detailed understanding. It relates also not just to retail but it is perhaps, where it comes into sharpest focus just how important it is to get right.

The pandemic that started in 2020 had a dramatic impact on the automotive industry. Sales of cars disappeared overnight as retailers were forced to close the supply chain as well as production and assembly plants were impacted by labor issues. Since 2021, it has allowed motor manufacturers to review their models and their markets. Holden, part of GM, retired from Australia and New Zealand, Mitsubishi announced it was "pulling back," from North America and left Europe altogether; Renault and Nissan agreed to divide up their respective markets rather than compete. Other companies took similar approaches to certain markets or certain products. All these decisions were based on market share, product rationalization, future potential, cost, and return. However, not all automotive decisions are thus.

In 2007, Suzuki entered the North American automotive (car) market. They were already well established there through their motorcycles and, as Japan's then fourth largest car manufacturer they had not only the financial muscle to edge their way in and survive but they also had a highly regarded brand and knew the territory. While it may be true that North American tastes and Japanese tastes in motor cars are different, that is much less the case today than in 1962 when GM produced 51 percent of all cars sold in the United States.

Honda entered the U.S. market in 1959 and by 2007 had revenues of $99 million. Suzuki accepted it would take a while to break into North

America, but they believed they had a good start and, in the XL7 a good car that would appeal to their new target market. The company did its homework and believed it had a product that fitted the needs of the buyer and knew much about the buyer (Cultural).

Suzuki until 2006 had a partnership with GM and had established an assembly plant in Canada for their new vehicle. Through their motorcycle division they knew the market well and combined they therefore believed they could manage the Administrative challenges that awaited them.

Geography was not an issue for Suzuki as they had a plant in the territory and much experience of managing complex supply chains and distribution channels—online, direct, and through dealerships. In addition, there was no issue with the Economic distance as they were already established in North America.

Toyota was selling around 100,000 Highlanders per annum in North America at the time Suzuki entered the market. It looked like an ideal market for a GM-based product with some unique features (e.g., a third row of seats) and from an established brand. Total sales in 2007 and 2008 were 22,761 and 22,548, respectively. In 2009, Suzuki declared it was leaving the market.

Despite Suzuki ticking all the boxes for a CAGE assessment, it lacked the one thing that this did not cover. The Suzuki XL7 was a good product but was not a standout product able to take on established products in a competitive market. Even when you do have a great product, it still does not guarantee success.

It need not be complex products that fail. Certain products and services are ubiquitous around the world, from waiting and hospitality to travel and transport. But, of all products and services perhaps the ones that are seen most globally are some basic staple foods and beverages. So, in July 2000 when Starbucks opened its first shop in Australia, it did not seem such a big leap.

Starbucks assessed that coffee is drunk everywhere and, aside for personal preferences and sourcing the right mix of key ingredients, it is a relatively simple concept and a simple brew. For Starbucks, Australia represented a more local expansion than some of its already international offerings and even the language and culture were very similar.

Australia offered one of the biggest markets for coffee in the world and one would think an organization such as *Starbucks* would be professional enough to really do its homework, understand the market, identify buying habits, cultural differences, flavors, and wants of the customers and, potentially, buy a local coffee shop or two and learn from them. Sadly, for *Starbucks*, although perhaps not the consumers, they simply looked at Australia as similar to the United States and, because of much of its recent heritage, Europe. It followed that copying what they had done before would simply work.

By late 2007, *Starbucks* had amassed 87 stores across Australia. Their financial muscle helped accelerate their expansion across this vast country and, with deep pockets they could weather the short-term financial losses. In the first seven years, these losses were estimated to be US$54 million.

What *Starbucks* missed was that Australians prefer independent, local chains. Also, *Starbucks* also was more expensive than small cafes. Eight years after it entered the market, Starbuck eventually gave up and closed 61 stores. That they stayed eight years is remarkable. Some years later, in 2014, *Starbucks* eventually learnt to adapt rather than admit defeat completely. Their last remaining outlets were handed over to *Withers Group* which, until 2019 owned *7-Eleven* in Australia. Accounts for 2020 show that *Starbucks* is still losing money in Australia.

When *Starbucks* entered China, it invested heavily in understanding Chinese family values and cultural norms of their new market. It tailored its offering not just the beverages but also how it managed its staff ("partners") and treated its customers. Knowing China was going to be different ensured *Starbucks* fully investigated and understood. Thinking Australia was the same as Europe and North America meant a lot less due diligence was done.

Not understanding the Environment into which you are going can be costly, and if *Starbucks* can get it wrong then so can anyone.

CAGE could be applied regionally as well as internationally. In countries as large as the United States, Russia, China, and India, there can be significant differences in many elements from one region or state to another. Indeed, even climate can have an impact, so it could be you want to apply the CAGE Distance Framework to not just international expansion.

Product Development

Creating new products and services to appeal to the existing market or client base is an effective way to expand the product portfolio. The challenge often is finding the right product that complements the existing product and does not cannibalize the existing revenue streams.

The most obvious way to achieve this is to develop new products or services but this requires research and development and does not guarantee success. Acquisition of rights to produce another company's products or to secure rights to sell in your region or territory is a way to acquire a new product without the R&D. However, as we have seen, the success of a product or service in one market does not guarantee the same in another.

Of course, buying a competitor that has a broader product range or buying a company that has a divergent range but one that sits well in your market could also prove beneficial.

Apple went from developing desktop computers to laptops, phones, personal devices, wearables, and much more. Away from the hardware side, they have developed significant revenue streams in application downloads and music streaming services. By evolving the brand and by adding products incrementally that have created a loyal customer base eager for the next product.

Diversification

We have mentioned taking an existing product to a new market or tasking a new product to the existing market. But taking a new product to a new market is extremely high risk and rarely done. It has succeeded but rarely.

The *Colgate* brand is well known, the true pioneers of toothpaste. In 1982, *Colgate Palmolive*, under the *Colgate* brand, introduced frozen ready meals. Perhaps they were trying to stimulate demand for their main product! Of course, it did not work.

Where the brand name is powerful it can work. *Virgin Group* has diversified into many different products and services appealing to different markets. In the UK *Tesco*, a food retailer, branched out into various financial services, mobile phones and is always looking to diversify further.

Brand value and customer loyalty can help significantly when companies develop new product offerings. For most companies, there is only a certain amount of brand stretch. Had *Tesco* offered banking services in the 1960s it would most likely have failed, who would trust a grocery store with their savings and investments?

Understanding what is possible in terms of stretching your customers to buy new products or services requires an understanding of your clients and the way they buy and what else they may be willing to buy.

A client of mine had run a successful commercial cleaning and maintenance company. It had grown over several years and had achieved great success in a large part of the UK. It had acquired competitors either to remove the competition or to grow their client list and order-book. However, the next step was more challenging.

To continue in their chosen field and expand further geographically would pose a logistical challenge for them and their in-house supply chain as well as push their flexible part-time and contingent workforce even farther afield.

We proposed they buy several small, local office supply companies. This would complement their product offering and not challenge their geographical scope. They were already used to dealing with the buying departments of their clients and had several regional and local governmental organizations as well as multiple medium-sized commercial businesses. This approach would allow them to grow their revenues and profits, whilst not challenging their regional structure. It would strengthen their existing relationship with their buyers too.

The Ansoff Matrix is a relatively simple model that, perhaps, does not suit well the complex businesses of today. As a result, you may see a developed version of the Matrix where it is not simply a 2×2 matrix of yes or no but something with a more granular view of the options open to a company. An example of this is the Expansion and Diversification market strategies matrix, as demonstrated in Figure 2.6.

It is not uncommon that companies do not fully understand their product or service. It is also not uncommon for companies to undertake multiple market or product expansions/developments at the same time.

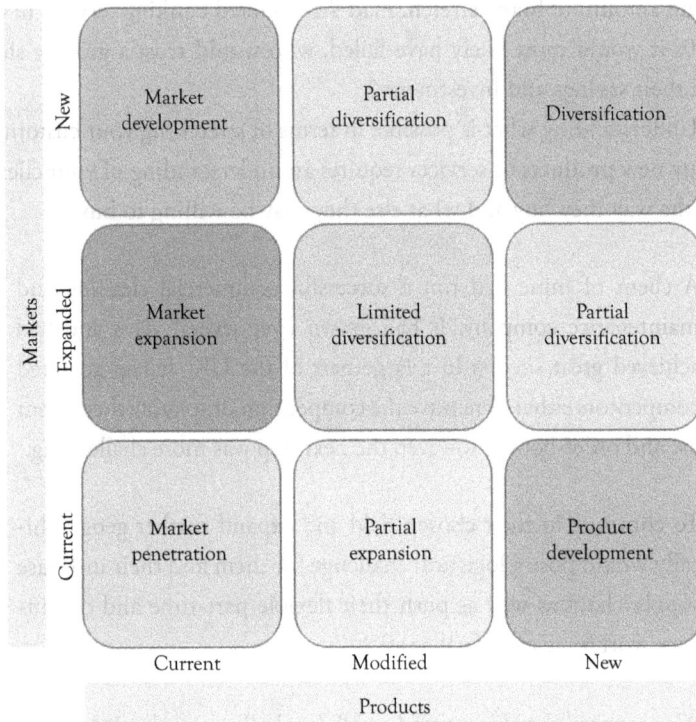

Figure 2.6 Expansion and Diversification market strategies

Equally not every foray ends in failure, but it is true that success is better achieved if you really understand your product and where you can take it, what you can do with it next.

Cross-Sell and Upsell

Cross-selling and upselling are as much about sales ability as product and product development. Neither of them fit well in the Ansoff Matrix but it would be remiss to leave them both out.

Cross-selling is when one product leads to another that is related and can be sold alongside. Upselling is when a better product is sold in replacement of the one the customer opted for first. It is an often-argued point whether Upselling and Cross-selling fit into Product Development or are outside the Ansoff Matrix. To my mind if you sell something in addition that is clearly Product more than Market development and if

Upselling then it is the same product to some degree just with a higher ticket price or better margin, or both.

Salespeople should be targeted on their Upsell and Cross-sell performance specifically, not just on new name business or account retention. Accepted it may not always be easier, or indeed always possible, but to ignore these two vital opportunities is to ignore the potential for improved sales performance.

How you target salespeople on Cross-sell and Upsell really depends on the product and services you sell.

Cross-sell may not happen immediately. As people moved to working from home more consistently in 2020, the demand for bigger monitors and laptops sharply increased. But this was long after the initial surge of demand for laptops and basic peripherals. The demand for additional equipment and even larger monitors maintained and other peripherals such as better audio recording and playback equipment continued to grow. Companies in the hardware supply industry focused first on satisfying the demand for new homeworkers and then began following up later, once people were established at home, to sell bigger and better hardware. The year 2020 began as a huge opportunity for new hardware and ended with a huge opportunity for Upsell and Cross-sell.

Key Takeaways

Product knowledge is a key part of any salesperson's arsenal. Not so much the detailed facts and figures rather how it benefits the end customer, how it compares the competition, and what USPs it brings to the conversation. Understanding the product or service allows the salesperson to elevate their offering above the rest. It allows the customer to make the decision in favor of our salesperson and it ensures that any later scrutiny supports the initial decision.

In the world of complex sales, marketing teams will spend considerable amounts of time developing competitor analysis reports. Often in the form of a simple chart to compare ours to theirs. Typically, these would be one per (major) competitor and perhaps a general report for the lesser competitors. Whether a SWOT (Strengths, Weaknesses, Opportunities,

Threats) Analysis or other should not matter if it serves the purpose of helping the salesperson present their product in an advantageous light.

Product knowledge is not just about the product or service as an island, as we have seen, but how it fits into the current market and whether it serves the needs and demands of the customer. Merely having the best product and significant market share is not sufficient. Understanding where the market is going and what the future looks like for the customer and for our product, and how these two align is important.

Understanding what differences there are between the market we serve today and where the customer wants to take it tomorrow also matter. Simply selling a solution in one territory or country that is ill-suited to another needs to be managed, either in how the solution is sold or in the future product roadmap. Tools such as Ansoff, BCG, and GE-McKinsey help us identify the state now as a potential strategy for tomorrow.

To know where the customer is heading and what they want from the future and being able to address that requires a detailed understanding of the product and the future of the product. The CAGE Distance Framework examples we have provided were international, but it can be easily applied to regional and even local markets.

Knowing product strengths and that of the competition are important. Knowing the future direction and potential of a competitor can be a hard question to answer. It matters that salespeople feedback what they learn and understand to their sales colleagues and to marketing to build a picture not just of the competitive landscape today but also of tomorrow. It also matters that the company uses simple tools to gather feedback and formulate an understanding and always stay one step ahead of the market.

Great salespeople spend time not to learn their product but to understand their product. They spend time understanding the competition and they invest in understanding the customer. They know not only what the customer wants but what the customer wants next or how to sell more. Where all these combine is where great salespeople shine and where deals are made bigger or are won and lost. It is not just enough to merely know your product anymore.

Sales Opportunity Management is a step-by-step approach moving from the first conversation through to sales success. It is a structured and disciplined approach led by the salesperson. Without a good understanding of our product strengths and weaknesses and that of the competition, and without an understanding of the needs of the customer and the market means even the best management of a sales pursuit will fail. Sales Opportunity Management cannot operate effectively as a standalone process, detached from the customer needs.

CHAPTER 3

Sales Opportunity Management

Overview

The sale, from start to end, is a series of steps and check gates that the salesperson takes the potential customer. However, each sale, though it may sit alone as an island, is part of a bigger picture where all the sales are managed, and the right resource used to focus on the deals that offer the greatest return and the best chance of winning. There may always be outliers, whether that are Hail-Mary passes or an open goal with no keeper, but for the most part a win requires a good understanding of our attack, the competition's attack, and the customer's defense.

The focus of this chapter is about the corporate being, why they wield such influence and why that is important. Often salespeople see forecasting and budgeting as a necessary but undesirable part of the job. It may have been Kimi Räikkönen who said *"Leave me alone, I know what I'm doing"* but every salesperson has said it, or at least thought it, many times in their career.

Tools and systems exist to ease the burden of managing multiple opportunities. Salespeople may not always see it that way and, in some organizations, the scales tip the other way as a whole industry is built up around reporting and managing. There needs to be a balance between the company being in control and the salesperson being allowed to focus on the most critical part of their role. Some companies have got it right, many have not.

Critically, management and reporting need to be effective. Not effective in generating reports, but effective in generating the type of activities and attitude required to be successful. Goodhart's Law states *"When a measure becomes a target, it ceases to be a good measure."*

If a measure of success is 80 percent win rate then salespeople will only enter sales pursuits with a good chance of a win. A lot of useful data on lost deals will not be applied to the opportunity management systems. If salespeople are expected to close three deals a week then they may well close three, sandbagging the fourth for next month, or heavily discounting one to hit quota rather than playing the longer game for better margin.

This chapter looks at the need for sales forecasting and the impact it can have for the company and, therefore, why it is so important. Unlike most parts of any business, which has an ongoing process, levels of consistency and repeatability, and very few peaks and troughs; sales is different.

According to the Cambridge Dictionary, a Project is defined as *"a piece of planned work or activity that is completed over a period of time and intended to achieve a particular aim."* It follows an opportunity to win a new piece of business (a sale) is, therefore, a project. Here, then is the challenge. A sale has a start and an end, at the end of the pursuit it has an impact right across the business. Forecasting matters and can have implications far and wide, but having the correct measures should benefit the business, not be a process of itself to simply apply a Key Performance Indicators to salespeople who now adjust their performance to hit the target.

Management of the Each Opportunity

Sales Opportunity Management wraps around each sales pursuit. It provides the framework that allows the company to decide which sales to try and win and which to not pursue; when to stay on, when to quit. Done well it allows informed decision making, done poorly it can cost the company. Sales Opportunity Management is a vital and necessary part of the process.

Sales Opportunity Management is the game plan. Like all game plans, it is open to the sales team to deliver. However, it also relies on the opposition, or customer as we prefer to call them, to play the game too and abide by the rules. Game plans are subject to change as the game evolves and, occasionally, players may decide they know better than the coach. Side-lining players or even getting sent to the sin-bin can all happen in the pursuit of a sale.

In 1999, a group of four people got together in San Francisco to build what they described at the time a product for "salesforce automation." In truth, it did not automate the salesforce, but it did create a kernel for the sales process to sit around. By 2020, *Salesforce.com Inc.* was a $17 billion company.

Today we call these systems as CRM. They do not, in truth, for almost every user and user-company, manage the customer relationship rather they manage the sales process and marketing, which are a central resource for all that matters with regards the sales opportunity. As for the "automation," there are many salespeople who will say that CRM systems have not automated anything, but it has certainly created a whole lot more work!

CRM systems are, today, a vital tool for large organizations and small businesses alike. They allow us to coordinate data and work systematically in a way that makes us more focused and more efficient.

Contact Management

Sometimes referred to as people management but this could be confused as to the people working at the company as well as the customer people, so Contact Management seems more appropriate.

In 1956, Hildaur Nielsen filed a patent in the United States for a rotary card filing device thus paving the way for the first Contact Management system. From 1960s, a rotary card-based system, the *Rolodex*, would have been the must-have desk accessory. Replacing the then outdated *Zephyr American Autodex.*

As technology advanced, this became automated, first perhaps through simple flat databases (spreadsheets) and now to more sophisticated tools. However, whether it is a rotating card system, a spreadsheet, or a well-thumbed address book it still does the job. Modern technology has, however, allowed these humble devices to develop into altogether more sophisticated tools.

Managing contacts begins with a few basic, and obvious, elements: name, address, e-mail, phone, and so on. In the Business-to-Consumer (B2C) world, these would often be a mix of home (e.g., address) and perhaps work (e.g., phone number). For B2B, typically these are all work related although personal mobiles, as an example, may form part of the basic contact information.

For B2C, perhaps spouse, family, and other details may be required. However, for B2B it can get a whole lot more complex. Perhaps company information, or organization, parent company, department, and so on. Then responsibility, both functional and geographical. Add to this their relationship to other contacts and it can soon become a large task to gather all the data. While it may not be critical to capture every element—and often data can be bought or captured from elsewhere—a gap in knowledge (data) at a critical time may be the undoing of an opportunity.

Contact information should be stored in a structured and organized way. As more information becomes available, contact information can be amended and updated. Often the sources of information are from marketing campaigns, events, meetings, and third-party sources.

Information such as birthdays, names of assistants, hobbies, and so on while helpful to have and give a more rounded view of contacts can also be time consuming and unnecessary. If you have the data then use it, keep it updated, and always evaluate the need for the data and the benefits it gives versus the time and effort to maintain.

Collecting and keeping the data that will help you is a good thing, a necessary thing. Understanding who the contact is and some key pieces of information is essential. In addition to all this, you might also want to keep note of their disposition to your company and products, and indeed the views of your competitors.

Keeping customer contact information up to date is important. It is the launchpad for any campaign or marketing effort. It provides insight and clues to navigate the sales process. Plus, it allows you to track their career progression and follow them to new opportunities or engage when there are changes to or within an organization.

Contact Management works on multiple levels in B2B. It is not just the individual but the company they work for, their colleagues and associates and the hierarchy that binds them. The "tip of the spear" in any engagement may be one individual but you need to have a degree of understanding of the rest to be successful.

Buying roles exist in any large organization, whether they are influencers, evaluators, or users and whether they have budget or delivery responsibility. Working across the buying roles are buyer behaviors, which have varying degrees of influence.

According to Miller Heiman

Understanding your current position means knowing who all your key players are, how they feel about you, how they feel about your proposal, what questions they want to have answered, and how they see your proposal vis-a-vis their other options

To understand this and the varying options that follow, what corrective actions to take, what is working and what is not, what changes need to be made to personnel, product, or service and how to improve the gap you have, or catch up, against the competition can be quite complex. Having an effective contact management system helps.

Today the updated version of the book "New Strategic Selling" has many competitors, most notably "The Challenger Sale." However, even "Challenger" recognizes the different buyer personas and different levels of influence each may wield. In the main, there are four buying influences.

The Economic Buyer, who has overall control of the budget. Specifically, budget for the project, not perhaps company financial oversight and approval. Very often the CFO or FD may not be the Economic Buyer who have already approved the budget for department expenses. Where expenditure is sizeable it may require a committee, in this case the committee becomes the Economic Buyer. Or perhaps once a decision has been made, there is still a final internal (purely financial) sign-off with perhaps the finance department of the procurement team. In such a case, the approval committee is not the Economic Buyer, rather the recommender.

User Buyers can often be overlooked in large or complex sales. Selling a new system to the IT Department or the Head of Operations may seem the obvious choice, but the team that implements and then runs the system has influence too. If the system is overly complex or has elements that make it more difficult for the users then it can be derailed through the process of implementation or after and the cost to the salesperson's post implementation support team can become onerous.

Technical Buyers are very often gatekeepers and seen not so much as people that can approve, rather people that can kill a project or change of supplier. Getting the Technical Buyer onside ensures there are no later surprises that are beyond the control of the salesperson.

Technical Buyers will compare the proposed sale to doing it in-house, or do-nothing/remain the same. They will look at how the solution works and dovetails into other systems and processes, how it integrates, whether it complies to current policy and so forth. Technical Buyers should be viewed as never saying "yes" but can only say "no."

Finally, **The Coach**. Every company selling into an organization will have a Coach. Some Coaches will back more than one company in the race to be the new supplier. A Coach can feed information to their preferred supplier(s), and sometimes disinformation too! While Coaches are required to operate within the bounds of the law and of their employers' codes of conduct and ethics, it does not always follow that all Coaches behave thus.

Having a Coach in a position of influence, of course, matters. However, very often those with less to gain from their employer, may have more to gain personally, either through later influence or through potential future career options. A Coach may also hold another Buyer Influence.

Contact Management allows salespeople, sales management, and the wider sales team to understand the role and position of each person in the sales process, both from their functional position as well as their attitude and position within the sales pursuit itself.

Contact Management when done badly focuses on the more structured elements of data and focuses on the rigidity of functional organization and hierarchy. It does not consider the changes of influence and general attitude of each person or department to the salesperson, their product, and their company.

Done well, Contact Management goes beyond the functional and builds a complex profile of the task at hand, the teams of people within the sales pursuit and the roles, beliefs, and attitudes of each individual within the pursuit.

Opportunity Workflow Management/Automation

The production of anything requires several elements, raw resource, target end and, in-between a whole load of technology, systems, processes, and people. The humble junior school play needs all of these, and more. Without the right process, you will never get all the children rehearsed enough and without the right process management on the night it may still succeed but dare you take the chance?

In the world of sales, it could sometimes be said salespeople behave worse than prepubescent children, at least for some of the time, so having a system that works will help. In addition, automating much of that will help doubly so.

Managing an Opportunity requires not just the salesperson to manage it but a series of referees and umpires. Some of these are systems such as qualifying tools and some people, such as the Sales Manager. Without some form of management, preferably with automation, it is not Sales Opportunity Management, rather it becomes Open Hunting Season with no rules and kill as much as you like, even if you do not need it and cannot eat it.

Management of the sales opportunity needs to track and align with the process that the customer has. Not all prospective new customers have the same process but there are, in complex sales, a generally recognized set of steps. In any pursuit, some may take a much more significant role than others, some may appear at different stages, and some may not be called on at all, but to have a plan that aligns our sales pursuit with their buying process is the best place to begin a sales pursuit.

The chart (Figure 3.1) maps a standard process that a client may go through when buying a complex or large product or service. Indeed, for many of us we do these ourselves, perhaps with a little less staccato, when buying something as simple as a new domestic appliance.

It does not follow that this is always the process nor that every step is followed, but as a rule we should align our sales process to run alongside the prospect's buying process.

Initial contact

Research

Internal review

Introductory call

Capability
discussion

Qualifying
questions

Draft requirements

Demo/meeting

Observations

Shortlist and
proposal

Negotiation

Contract discussion

Agreement

Sign

Delivery

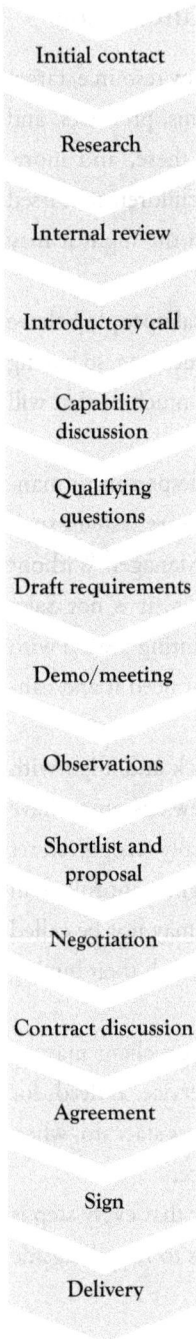

Figure 3.1 The
standard buying
process

In the last 30 years or so, nothing much has changed in this process, save for the research stage. Before the emergence of the Internet as a business tool and reliable search engines, research was often done at the behest of the client in favor of the suppliers. Perhaps asking for documents and evidence or in meetings. Today that tends to be done in isolation from the seller.

Moving the discussions at the early stages to online research removes the opportunity for the salesperson to shape the thinking of the buyer and to influence their needs. It also allows the buyer to go into much more detail or to dictate the value attached to each feature or function on their own terms. Online research has tipped the balance more in favor of the buyer and allowed them to become more knowledgeable more quickly. Accepted this affects all sellers equally and it means the bar has been raised for the salesperson right from the start.

It is not just the research where salespeople have little or no control. Throughout the sales pursuit, there are always factors you cannot control. Do not try to control them. *The Challenger Sales Model* emphasizes Teach, Tailor, and Take Control. In this situation, taking control is about what they can teach the client and not about what cannot be changed.

The Challenger Sales Model is complex and, can at times, be a dangerous tool. Well-trained and very often seasoned salespeople can attempt to embrace the Challenger model only to see it go awry. As the salesperson tries to teach the client and take control without the client being open to the change that was about to be imposed on them.

For things you cannot control that have a high chance of occurring, have a plan to deal with them.

Do not have a plan for every scenario and every likelihood that will make you less efficient and give you less time for more sales pursuits.

Salespeople can get knocked sideways because of something out of their control. It is typical to have an emotional reaction, but great salespeople instead focus on the process and let the feelings go. Looking at how to recover and regain an advantage. If a company loses a deal because of something outside its control they need to assess whether they knew and carried on in hope or whether it really was something unforeseen. Learn and move forward.

The biggest thing we cannot control is time; the amount of time we have available to purse the number of deals, the time the client takes to decide, and the time from start to end. Accepting you cannot control these, but you can certainly influence them will make a big difference to your productivity. Pushing a client that will not budge their timeline is wasteful of effort and may count against you, but that does not mean you let them drive the entire process and dictate the pace; there needs to be a balance and you need to challenge them to push ahead all the time.

Good salespeople are great at spotting early the deals that will close quickly and be relatively light touch in terms of effort, versus those that will drag on and require multiple and often repeat steps. It is a skill, like any other, that can be developed over time. How to understand this can be achieved through good qualifying, good sales management, and understanding the client and all the players within the process.

Most sales end when you lose. For every sale that a company wins, there are multiple losers. When you choose to lose is down to you and whether you pursue the opportunity to the end or resign earlier to focus on other deals is down to the salesperson and, very often, the Sales Manager.

Recognizing that a lost sale is not completely lost, even after the event, can be a dangerous belief. However, that does not mean you should quit on the spot and never engage with the client again. Timing is very often a key part of the decision-making process and, it could be that timing was not right this time but when the contract comes up for renewal in three years' time things may have changed. Between now and then does not require a huge investment of time but occasional reminders and updates, adding them to your quarterly newsletter, and so on may all be useful again in the future.

Perhaps contact the client part way through implementation if it is a big project and ask them how it is going. Ask for referrals. It amazes me how many salespeople lose a deal and never ask for a referral. If you had a good relationship with the buyer, it is likely they will have some sympathy for you and if they liked your product too then why would they not want to help you? We seem to believe referrals are part of the spoils of the winner, which is not the case.

A sales pursuit is never the same twice. That does not mean it follows the same pattern and may have many of the same elements and traits. Knowing how to win at sales requires several soft skills, tools, and techniques. Aligning the pursuit process with the plan, the buyer ensures we stay in step and are able to control everything on our side to match everything on theirs.

Sales Forecasting and Budgeting

The importance of an effective Sales Forecast cannot be understated. Sales Forecasting combines a way to increase the chances of success and reduce risk. More than that, however, it has impact right through the business:

- Forecasting helps determine production volumes and production mix. What products to produce and how many. This reaches as far as the supplier agreements and long-term forecasting.
- For the longer term, it influences R&D and new product development, as well as, potentially, discontinuing products.
- It feeds directly into the company's financial forecast.
- It can even impact decisions on company expansion, or retraction, new markets, and strategic direction of the company to certain markets and sectors.
- It directly impacts marketing spend, social media investment, and advertising focus, as well as direct customer-facing marketing and sales process spend.

All Sales Forecasts are wrong! However, getting it wrong does not mean attempts to have an accurate forecast should be ignored. Equally investing huge amounts of time to get marginal improvements in the forecast accuracy is also the wrong approach.

Even for the smallest of companies having an accurate sales forecast is important. Here it may be less about sales pursuits and strategies, marketing plans and CRM systems but something as simple as recent sales figures, previous seasonal sales figures, and a good stock take. For retailers it is perhaps referred to as stock control, but that still constitutes a sales forecast.

The Sales Forecasting process begins before the end of the previous year to create the next year budget. Reviews of overall results in terms of products and services sold, teams and individuals, and territories. From here, something that reflects a mix between what the company expects to achieve this year and the growth it expects to achieve next.

Anyone who has been in sales will tell stories where the budget is just imposed from above and is just 10 percent or more than the last year. Accepted there are companies where this is not far from reality and certainly. For some companies that next year's budget clearly bore no resemblance to what had happened previously, or to changes in the market, the competition, or product portfolio.

A good budget should challenge the entire company to deliver on target. It needs to be built with the entire company in mind. There is no point setting a budget if the supply chain or manufacturing cannot cope or if the demand does not exist.

Creating an accurate sales budget requires a structured approach. Taking historical trends and performance should be the baseline. Not the expected previous (or current) year but the actual. Understanding exceptional elements, such as socio-economic upheavals, freak weather, demographic changes, pandemics, and so on will allow you to adjust your baseline, considering the ongoing impact of such events or the likelihood of a repeat.

Adjustments are needed to the baseline for changes that you have implemented or that have impacted your customers and the marketplace. Understand pricing changes and customer changes. Major events, promotions, and competitive challenges for the next year should be factored in. Companies such as *Coca Cola* spend years planning for every Olympics. You may not be sponsoring the world's largest sporting event but the impact you can have in your sector can be significant if you plan to do something different.

Understanding market trends and how your competition will adapt and change over the next year affects your budget. Good market intelligence and good competitive intelligence are important in setting a budget.

Finally, look at the product changes you have made and the impact likely to come from your channel sales if you have them. Sales Channels are the online and indirect partnership models you use to generate and close sales. Losing Channel Partners or gaining new Channel Partners or changing your go to market channel model all need considering.

There is a good reason why a well thought out budget matters. It impacts the entire business planning process for the following year and the business plan for the next three or more. The simple notion of "last year plus 10 percent" may work for some top-down driven organizations but it should not.

In the first decade of the 21st century, we saw an ever-increasing glut of cars produced worldwide and a slowdown in demand and a change in buying habits as well as product demand changes. Manufacturers cannot easily shut down whole production lines or slow down lines easily. Nor can they easily switch from one model to another. This creates an over-supply, which has additional costs, storage, degradation, and so on. The global pandemic that started in 2020 helped by halting the production lines at least.

Amidst all this, there was a significant shift toward new powertrains, batteries, hybrids, and to some extent hydrogen. Some regions and sectors remained strong or grew but the overall trend was down and changing.

Prior to 2020, manufacturers set ever higher targets for retailers to sell the excess stock and retailers passed this on to their sales teams in the form of targets. A typical example of top-down target setting because of outside influences but without any regard for the impact these same influences were having.

What halted the constant growing mass production of cars that could not be easily sold was not a change in supply or demand but an altogether different and outside influence. The impact of Covid-19 allowed the industry time to adjust and change in a way previously thought impossible. Today car manufacturers are setting new targets to their retailers and there are new challenges both in the supply chain and changes in the products the consumer wants.

Having set the sales budget for the year, now we need to forecast. The size and nature of the pipeline and measures through the pipe as opportunities progress is a good place to start with forecasting. Certainly, a mathematical approach helps. However, for companies with small volume sales of high-value solutions, the difference between one win and loss can be huge. All companies will have their "whale hunters" and treating these differently may be required.

> The Chief Executive Officer of a company I was working for was visiting from the United States. He was meeting some of the team and asked for a meeting with me to discuss how we could expand the success we had achieved to date. During that discussion he complained that I was "a nightmare to manage"—he meant in terms of forecasting.

> At the time I did one or two deals a year, usually one. Each deal was, in USD, big-six or seven figures and with healthy margins. Deals would include a mix of software, partner-provided hardware, and part outsourced implementation. As a solution sale each proved very successful, and the process of implementation worked well, and every customer was willing to be a reference.

> The cost of sale was not particularly high, we had a very small team of sales and marketing, and a lot of the product development was shared across or sourced from other platforms.

> The CEO knew we would do a deal and hit our number. However, he never knew when that would happen, despite our best attempts at a forecast. If we did a second deal that took us way over sales budget it would make a big difference to our department and a reasonable difference to the company figures too.

> The CEO's "nightmare" was all around planning, not whether we would come out ahead at the end of the year, or whether the

department would fail its target. As a sales and marketing team we did our job well, but for the business they never knew when payday would be the big hit they wanted.

The company, like most software companies, now sells solutions as a service with a monthly fee for all-inclusive license, support, and hosting. Working at this company, forecasting the win or loss was not the problem, it was forecasting the demand for resources such as the data build and implementation team.

Having an accurate sales forecast is as important as a realistic yet stretching target or budget. However, in reporting against target you need to be accurate in what will come in and what is less likely to come in and to disqualify deals from your forecast that are outliers. Or potentially disqualify them altogether. Despite all this any sales forecast will be inaccurate anyway, how inaccurate depends on the process, methodology and honesty of the information put into the process.

In companies, where large volumes of small sales, such as High Street retail, are concerned a sales forecast is an altogether different process to a smaller company selling high-value solutions, such as high-end furniture retail. For example, the way *Ikea* forecasts sales is wholly different to the way *Savoir Beds* conducts a forecast.

A sales forecast should be for the next month or quarter or until year end and, possibly, for next year. It should include sales achieved to date. Good forecasters look back at the year so far and the outcome achieved versus what was expected. This is then reflected in the probability going forward. In truth most companies, at the sales team level, do not do this but some, at senior management level, may.

Including performance of year to date against expected achievement allows us to understand what is happening in the marketplace. If, for example, a company typically wins three deals in five but is consistently now winning only two of every five then a change has happened with us, our competitor, demand, the market generally. Applying a factor across future forecasts to take this into account will help get an accurate forecast. However, just make sure that it is done only once, we do not want the sales team taking a pessimistic view of the year ahead for senior management to then apply a discount on the forecast as well.

There are multiple reasons why a sales forecast is never totally accurate. The most usual of these is down to an excess of optimism by the salesperson. Almost all salespeople are ever optimistic, it is in their nature. As a result, sales dates slip because the Sales Manager was pushing the salesperson to close the deal and the salesperson backed themselves to get it over the line as requested. Accepted there may be outside influences that cause last-minute delays but, for the most part, sales tend to run to process, certainly in large and complex deals.

Sales teams are under pressure to maintain a healthy pipeline and some within the team may pad out their forecast with deals that will never come in. Either because they genuinely believe the deal will deliver or they just need the numbers to look good. In either case, it is a way a salesperson can manage local pressure, but it does little to help the eventual sales numbers and to help the company plan.

I was working at an outsourcing company, and we had our monthly sales review. All the team were present, along with the regional Sales Manager and the Vice President of Sales. In typical fashion we discussed what we were seeing in the market, people were asked to discuss their hot prospects and the team also put forward opportunities where they needed some help or advice.

Toward the end of the meeting the VP put up a slide showing the win rate. It looked very healthy and clearly the team was excellent at closing deals. The VP, however, saw it differently and accused the sales team of not working hard enough to generate new opportunities. In short, we were not prospecting hard enough.

About three months later, maybe more, at another sales team meeting we went through the same process, buoyed by an increasingly successful year in won business and the chance of almost all hitting target. The Sales Manager then presented a slide explaining that senior management wanted to know why our win-rate had dropped and despite still being on target by winning as many deals but now we were losing more deals as well.

Sometimes, the same data can be read in different ways by different managers. Every company wants salespeople to prospect for new opportunities, but they also want a healthy win-rate.

Not all sales forecast issues are down to overpromise or failure to close. Sometimes deals are won that were unexpected or that suddenly come forward. These "blue sky" deals that were not forecast can be great for salespeople, and especially their bonus, but they do not help with forecast accuracy, unless you were already behind on forecast of course. That is, assuming the new deals won are similar in nature to the ones that did not come through.

Some salespeople will keep deals quiet or play them down to keep them off the management radar. Known as "sandbagging" it gives the salesperson an opportunity to save face if another deal fails and means there is less chance of a sales target adjustment if they are perceived to be overachieving their target.

Not all salespeople have the same behavior. Some will be far more optimistic and win fewer deals as a percentage when compared with their colleagues. Some will prospect harder, qualify less, and win more as a percentage where others will purse more deals and have a lower win-ratio. As a Sales Manager understanding the individual forecasts of each team member will allow for a more accurate combined forecast.

Even the terminology will vary between salespeople. What some consider a qualified opportunity, others may consider it not yet sufficiently qualified. Having the same terminology does not mean they are interpreted in the same way by all salespeople.

Regardless of how accurate you want your sales forecast to be, remember, it is just a report. In some larger organizations, Sales Managers have been known to spend up to 10 percent of their working week chasing salespeople for updates, challenging their numbers, reworking the figures, and then presenting the results. Far too much time on telling people what may be about to happen rather than making it happen.

Spending time identifying those pursuits that have a small chance of happening and working them less and focusing real time and effort on those with the highest chance of delivering the greatest benefit. This should be the focus of any salesperson. In doing so, and scoring the opportunities accordingly, your sales forecast accuracy will also improve.

The final reason why sales forecasts are inaccurate is down to the customer itself. Despite the very best intentions, the best sales process, and best sales team the process is still one the customer has ultimate control over. Even after signature, the deal may not go ahead. Changes within the company or the market may impact sales or simply the salesperson was being led along to give the customer leverage against their preferred vendor.

Sales forecasting is not a simple process of weighing up the number of deals in the pipeline and the win rate multiplier. Complex sales forecasting requires a weighted scoring against each opportunity depending on several parameters, not least of which is where it is in the Sales Funnel.

Key Takeaways

Understanding that Sales is a project (Chapter 1) with a series of key steps, qualifications and has go/no-go gates is fundamental to understanding how to have effective Sales Opportunity Management. As with any project there needs to be a Project Manager (the salesperson), the Client (Customer), and the Project Sponsor (Sales Manager). Other roles exist too as in any project but these three are critical to the success of the sales pursuit (project).

These additional roles exist within the company target itself in the form of different buyer personas. Understanding the role of the buyer personas and who is undertaking them may not always be easy or obvious. In addition, each buyer will have their own bias toward the supplier or solution or simply to do nothing or resist change. Sales is far more chess or cricket than it is kayaking or skiing.

Having the discipline within the process, and of the salesperson, to clearly identify the key elements that will constitute success and avoid surprises will reduce wasted time and cost on fruitless pursuits and allow greater focus on those with a greater chance of a win. At this point it is also worth mentioning, not all deals are worth winning. If the cost to win or serve outweighs the gains then it may be good for market share or as a publicity claim but what is the impact of not investing time in that pursuit versus another, more profitable one. Indeed, the company may not have sufficient resources to pursue all the deals on the table.

Sales discipline has a dramatic impact on the effectiveness of marketing, and vice-versa. What content the marketing team needs to produce and what of the 9 Ps have the greatest significance for the customer can be lost in a flurry of noise and lack of clarity from sales.

While the sales process the client goes through will vary from client to client, product to product, core elements remain. It may be simpler or even more involved but, as a project checklist it provides a valuable tool to measure progress and gauge likelihood of success.

Numerous books on sales techniques have been written, some referenced in this book. Knowing what works for each salesperson is where to begin but, as with any skill, consistent training and development is needed. This can take the form of general development or specific skills required. The Challenger Sales Model was first developed in 2011 and Miller Heiman's Strategic Selling in 1945. Perhaps that reflects the changing culture of sales, or the changing culture of society. However, both serve well the needs of salespeople and, perhaps rather than competing, they provide complimentary sets of tools to be used.

More focused texts and training can be used to work on presentation skills or closing techniques, questioning, and qualifying. As with any good sports person working on the areas where there are skills deficiency is what separates those that made it to the big arenas and those that did not.

In sales, there should be no surprises. Everything should be under control and all likely scenarios understood in advance. Constant liaison with marketing to feedback progress or call for content can only be done if the salesperson is in the driving seat and has a plan. Sales may be the driver but marketing is the navigator with the pace-notes.

Surprises not only make it hard for companies to manage but they also undermine the credibility of the salesperson and, to a lesser extent, the Sales Manager for not also being aware. We may think of salespeople as creative, even flamboyant, and indeed perhaps in personality that is true, but salespeople must be the most organized, methodical, and disciplined people too. Anything less has fallout that creates ripples right across the business.

CHAPTER 4

Marketing

Overview

In a book on sales, one may be given for thinking Marketing is a different subject. In business, these two often sit as distinctly different teams with different management and, it may feel, with different objectives.

Whenever Marketing is combined with Sales, it is almost always referred to as "Sales and Marketing" yet for almost every part the process and handoff between Marketing to Sales is the other way around. Sales and Marketing are also often viewed, rightly, as squabbling siblings. Saying the other was to blame for failure and claiming the credit for when things go well.

While Marketing and Sales very often work as a well-oiled machine of two parts, the rivalry can lead to problems between the two. Managed well, Marketing and Sales combine to achieve greatness. Left unattended it can lead to conflict of objectives and, therefore, less than fully productive.

For anyone in Sales, it matters to understand what Marketing can do to help the sales pursuit. What tools and techniques Marketing use to better understand the field of play and help the salesperson understand rules of the game and just how far to bend them. It may be that Sébastien Ogier won the World Rally Championship in 2021 but it was not him that built or maintained the car or that read the pace notes. In fact, it was a French driver and co-driver, with a Japanese car, built and maintained by a team from Finland.

The 7 Ps of the Marketing Mix have been around for 30 years but I would argue that now needs updating to add Partnership and Planet. That the Marketing Mix is studied by business students around the globe demonstrates its importance. That it is called the Marketing Mix and not the Sales & Marketing Mix shows who is really in the driving seat or determining how any salesperson with their products and services toolkit should enter the fray.

Today, customers are much more self-serving. Relying on salespeople to educate the client on what options are available and the product or service for sale has been replaced extensively by the client researching online, reading reviews, and asking other customers for their thoughts. The ability to have more input from more people has now tipped the balance away from the influence of the salesperson to the influence of the masses.

As the balance has shifted so too has the importance of getting the message out to the potential client earlier and in a more informed way through a more varied content. And now, rather than educating the customer at the start, Marketing is educating the customer further into the process and also making sure they stay loyal after the sale is won and use postsale as an opportunity to build greater loyalty and also win more new business.

Marketing is a critical partner to Sales of that there is no doubt and has become more so in recent years. Sales not only needs Marketing but it needs Marketing to do more and be better than at any time before now.

The Marketing Mix

To understand the Marketing Mix, we first need to know what is meant by Marketing. For this we should turn to Dr. Philip Kotler; often referred to as the father of modern marketing. His book *Marketing Management* was first printed in 1967 and has had multiple reprints. He has written more than 55 books on the subject printed in more than 20 languages. According to Kotler:

> ... *the science and art of exploring, creating, and delivering value to satisfy the needs of a target market at a profit. Marketing identifies unfulfilled needs and desires. It defines, measures, and quantifies the size of the identified market and the profit potential. It pinpoints which segments the company is capable of serving best and it designs and promotes the appropriate products and services.*

That is quite a lot to take in from such a short paragraph.

For me, the key elements of this statement are that it identifies unful-filled needs or desires and then matches that to what the company could achieve once it understands the size of the opportunity. Needs and desires are quite different things, we may all need a car to get to work but it would be difficult to justify it has to be a *Ferrari*, when perhaps a *Toyota* will do perfectly well.

For marketing, the most used template is the Marketing Mix or 7 Ps. The Marketing Mix goes back to 1949 and was then the 4 Ps: Product, Price, Promotion, and Place (Figure 4.1).

Product is not just what you make, what services and products you provide, but how the product is perceived by the customer. A simple example, perhaps, the *Apple iPhone*. It competes against a range of alter-natives but has a very loyal following with customers who would not have anything else. People are deeply passionate about the *Apple iPhone*, and that is because the product is not just a phone as bought by the customer; it makes a statement, it is a lifestyle choice.

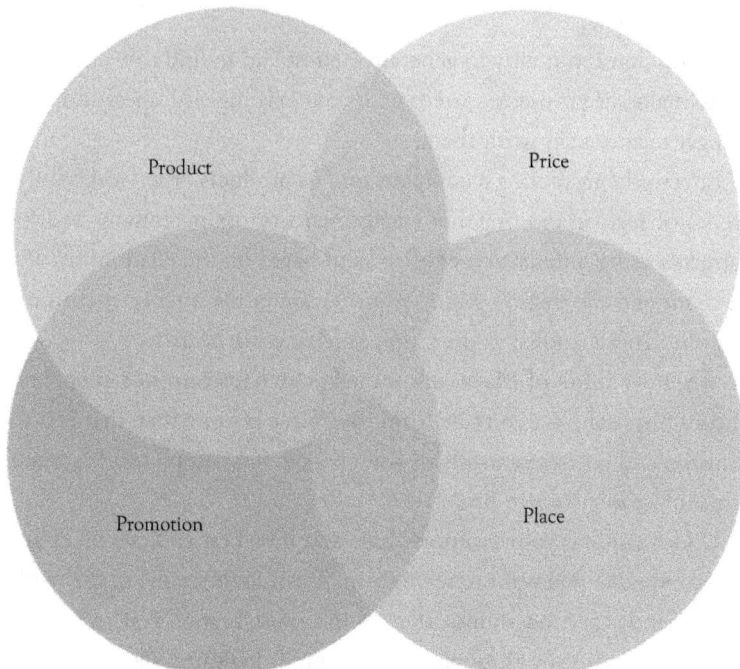

Figure 4.1 The Marketing Mix (4 Ps)

If you only ever compete on **price**, there is only one way and that is a race to the bottom. While you may want to offer a no-frills service, or an entry-level model price is about understanding what the customer is willing to pay for that service, not simply offering the product or service at rock-bottom price. Price has an upper level also and understanding how much the customer is willing to pay is also important for any pricing strategy.

Promoting products or services is a far more complex consideration than just advertising. During the global pandemic that started in 2020, many companies turned to promoting their products and services online. That it took a pandemic to start what should have already been in place should be worrying.

Beyond purely online promotion was the desire by many companies to offer free or heavily discounted products and services. For some services, this offered a "try before you buy" option but the balance of what was free and what had to be paid for slipped firmly in the direction of the buyer. Desperation set in for some companies and the drive was all about revenues to keep the company on life support. For some, this was still not enough.

Promotion is not only to generate interest and to find new clients but also to make sure you stay current with your existing customers and build stronger relationships with them.

Effectively promoting a company and its products or services requires a series of regular and ongoing engagements across potentially multiple platforms using different types of content based on the relationship with the client and the stage at which you/they are in the buying or customer life cycle. This is known as the Content Marketing Matrix.

When we think of **Place**, our thoughts perhaps turn to a shop or an office, a physical place to trade from. But Place is more than that it is the countries and territories in which you operate, it is our physical as well as virtual place or presence also.

Understanding your customer base and how best to serve them and, indeed, whether you want to serve them. The richest retailer in the world, until recently, had no shops. The world's most brand loyal technology company sells mainly through its own brand dedicated shops. But that does not mean change cannot happen or you get it right the first time, indeed often change can occur many years later.

Harrods, arguably the world's most famous shop, has stood alone in a part of West London since 1849. In recent times, it has opened stores at some UK airports. Now it is expanding with outlet stores, international airports, and other shops as well as working hard on its online presence. It was not that it took 150+ years to realize it had to change, more that it took until then for the owners to want to do that and the market conditions for it to work.

Place is, as we have shown, where you trade from. It is also where you trade to. Deciding to go into a market is as much about market opportunity as it is cost of entry and competitive situation.

In 2020, after 10 years of trying, *Harley Davidson* finally pulled out of the Indian market. The world's largest motorcycle market did not offer enough of a return for the iconic brand. It closed its factory and laid off all its staff. Ten years was perhaps long enough to give it a go. Whether the brand was right for that market is questionable based on the competition and the average alternative cost but at least they tried. For *Harley Davidson*, the product was great, the market potential was huge but it just was not the right marketplace for them to be.

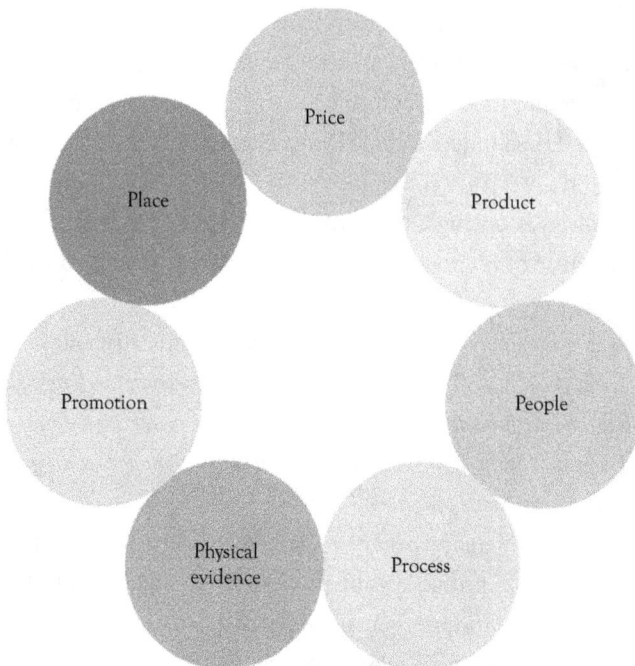

Figure 4.2 The Marketing Mix (7 Ps)

In the 1980s, the 4 Ps, the Marketing Mix, became the 7 Ps. We added People, Process, and Physical evidence, see Figure 4.2.

Let us be clear. It is the **People** who make the product, it is the People who deliver the product, it is the People who sell the product, and it is other People who supply the parts, support your business and other People that buy your product. People are, therefore, more than a little important to your business.

In an organization, there are productive and less productive people and, in complex assembly or manufacturing companies' productivity is only achieved at the rate of the lowest performing team/division/department. In absolute terms, therefore, productivity is often seen as relatively fixed but must be included in the People element, or perhaps we should add another "P."

The People and **Processes** influence how productive you can be in times of change. The ability to adapt and change, the ability to increase the quality or quantity of output, the ability to adapt to new trends, new markets, changing demand. These are all measures of the productivity of a company. In short, how much you can take an input, such as a change in market conditions, and adapt to it.

Good salespeople, good managers, indeed anyone in a business who is good at their job is usually an asset to the company. For those facing the customer and those responsible for making sure the right message is well delivered then indeed People form a vital part of the Marketing Mix.

People deliver the entire customer experience. Companies that pride themselves on high Net Promoter Scores (NPS) often see their success because of their wider team, not just those dealing directly with the customer.

NPS is a tool to measure customer loyalty and satisfaction. According to Satmetrix *"NPS®, measures customer experience and predicts business growth. This proven metric, based on years of research, transformed the business world. Today, it provides the core measurement for leading customer experience management programs."*

NPS is the difference between the percentage of Promoters (people who will positively promote your product or company) and Detractors (people who will promote you in a negative way). For example, if 25 percent of your customers would positively promote your product or service or company, 55 percent of people are neither avidly for or against ("Passive"), and 20 percent are Detractors, the NPS will be +5. With a maximum of 10, any high value positive number is particularly good.

For any company to thrive, particularly one that is growing or one that has scale, good, efficient processes are vital. They enable the company to operate efficiently. They remove some of the cost. And they also enable you to respond quickly to changes within the customer demand, or potentially what the competition is doing.

Processes allow the company to better respond to changing customer demands or needs, to react where there are challenges and opportunities and to ensure greater efficiency and, therefore, better serve the customer.

In marketing, Processes allow us to stay more in tune with the customer and allow the customer to work with us, the supplier in a way that is familiar to them. Perhaps more a hygiene factor than a true marketing element in that regard but, nevertheless, very important in our customer relationship.

The last of the 7 Ps is **Physical evidence**. The Physical element of the 7 Ps represents the environment where the customer experiences the supplier. This could be a shop or restaurant, perhaps even the delivery truck and way the parcel is left by your door.

Physical evidence is also about the brochures you leave behind, the business cards, staff uniforms and everything that has your brand, your image, or a physical representation of your company. Ironically for many companies nowadays Physical evidence is online and hardly physical at all. Not so much the online shop rather how you feel when you interact online.

The Physical side of the Marketing Mix explains why companies spend significantly to reduce the number of clicks for a checkout, look at layout and color palettes and, for the shop, hotel, restaurant, and so on why huge sums are spent on décor and why consistency of branding matter for multiple outlets, for marketing and sales material and why the best delivery companies pride themselves in clean vehicles and smart uniforms.

Today the 7 Ps may no longer be enough. This century has seen a seismic shift in our collective values. As the workforce changes and evolves this will only continue to evolve. For example, in Africa the number of people below 18 years of age is now greater than the entire rest of the population.

I would like to add two more to the Marketing Mix: Partnership and Planet and have demonstrated this in Figure 4.3.

In a world that is facing the challenges we have today we absolutely must consider **Planet** as an element of the Marketing Mix.

For most of us today we are acutely aware of the environmental impact we have on the planet and the impact of globalization. But it is not just complex and long supply chains that we need to consider. Packaging, for example, should be considered as should, potentially, the environmental impact of the company's suppliers and even its resellers and distributors.

Factoring in the environmental cost could impact quality and price. However, it also stimulates innovation, as we have seen most recently in the automotive industry. Where there is an additional cost, this may be passed onto consumers who are willing to pay more for products that are sourced in what they consider more ethical or less environmentally impactful ways.

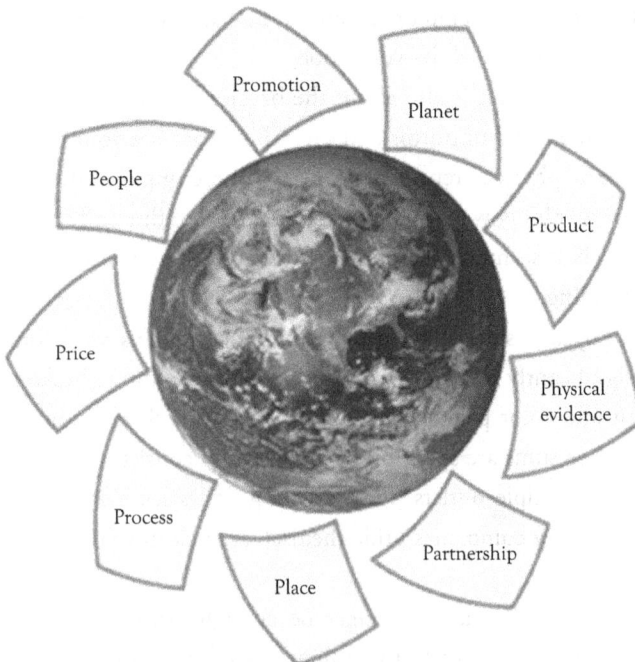

Figure 4.3 The Marketing Mix (9 Ps)

Taking this message to the consumer can add value to the company and could increase margins if done well.

Many companies are becoming more "eco-friendly" but doing so quietly as part of their social responsibility programs. While they may not directly use this for their marketing, it does have an impact overall and may form part of a more subtle and wider message about the company.

Often referred to as Green Marketing, products with sustainable attributes have been taking a larger share of sales. In the United States, this went from 19.7 percent in 2014 to 22.3 percent in 2017 and is still growing. Even though less than 20 percent of U.S. citizens consider themselves committed to environmental change.

That the environment is now recognized as a part of the Marketing Mix was first demonstrated in an article by environmentalist Jay Westerveld, back in 1986. At the time he was staying in a hotel where a sign in the bathroom encouraged him to reuse towels, to reduce the environmental impact of repeated washing. Westerveld considered the hotel's motives to be more about reducing cost (there was no discount for recycling towels in this way) and less about caring for the environment.

By comparison, a recent stay at the NH Hotel in Nice. For every day that I did not request new towels I received a complimentary drinks voucher to the rooftop terrace. This was not promoted in advance of my booking, nor is it mentioned on their website. The hotel is committed to a better environmental footprint clearly but does not feel the need to boast about it. Perhaps, in that way it works better? Certainly, it makes for a stronger recommendation by their guests rather than a pure marketing activity.

While consumers are becoming more environmentally aware, the drive for Green Marketing will continue. *Greenwashing* may not go away but perhaps becomes more difficult to hide.

Companies do not sit in a vacuum. Traditionally they would rely on suppliers and perhaps distributors. Today's modern companies will typically have an array of suppliers, multiple outlets, direct or otherwise and other partners deeply involved in their supply chain.

Partnerships should be added to the Marketing Mix not just because they have a direct influence on other elements of your company performance and sales/marketing capability but because they also directly reflect on the quality of your product and, very often, the values and standards of your company. Sourcing the best raw materials has an impact on the finished product and may even be something you want to promote, for example where you source your coffee beans and under what type of contract, for example, Fairtrade.

Partnerships are also reflected in your supply chain, perhaps the final leg delivery or even indirect sales agents and companies. If your delivery agent is underperforming or you have a rogue indirect sales channel, this will all directly impact on the company regardless that it is not the company itself. Similarly, being associated with the right Partners can have significant benefits in terms of your brand value or the overall performance of the business operations.

The Marketing Mix has evolved since it was first proposed and will, no doubt, continue to evolve, as all good models should (see Figure 4.4). Whether your preference is for 4 Ps, 7 Ps, or now 9 Ps perhaps reflects on the organization, your products, and markets as much as it does your own preference. However, in whatever form you choose, the Marketing Mix is a vital part of understanding any company's marketing strategy.

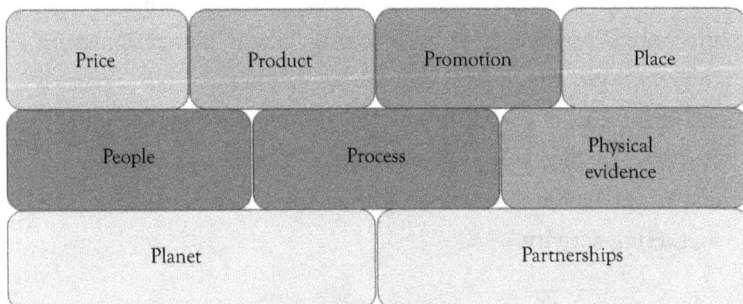

Figure 4.4 Evolution of the Marketing Mix

Content Marketing

Content Marketing aims to entertain, inspire, educate, and convince people to buy your product or service. In the pandemic that started in 2020, there was an upsurge in Content Marketing as companies went online to promote their goods and services as they had never done before, and social media and online marketing became a very noisy place. To stand out companies moved away from, or added to, their direct marketing messages with a range of new and original content.

The Content Marketing Matrix (see Figures 4.5 and 4.6) is an effective way to explain the various elements that make up Content Marketing. Not all the individual elements you may want to consider and for the simplest of products and sales providing rich content may be difficult anyway.

In terms of the buying cycle of customers typically the journey would start on the left-hand side of the matrix, where we Entertain them and educate them. We may do these at different times and, of course, in different ways, but we can also sometimes combine the two. A simple podcast or video interview with a subject matter expert can be both informative and entertaining.

Sponsoring a sports team is a great way to engage potential customers of the future. It can also underpin company values and engage the customer in ways more than entertainment alone. *M&M's* sponsorship of Nascar certainly creates interest with, not just the branding, but the livery itself. It gets potential customers interested in its product. Some industries and customer types work better for this type of advertising. *Visa's* involvement with the International Paralympic Committee, by comparison, is much less visible but says more about their company values than *M&M's* sponsorship package.

We want to entertain the potential customer so they like us and so we can build a rapport with them, usually through social media or advertising. The *Coca Cola* Christmas truck for example is, to many children entertaining as it signals Christmas is not far away. It is of course brand promotion in its most basic form too.

If we simply entertain our potential clients but do not educate them the journey to a successful sale becomes harder. In complex sales, there is usually a process where, as we progress through the sales pursuit, the amount of detail and the format or style of the content changes also. For example, a simple infographic is useful at the start of the education process, but later customers may need fact sheets or product sheets and white papers.

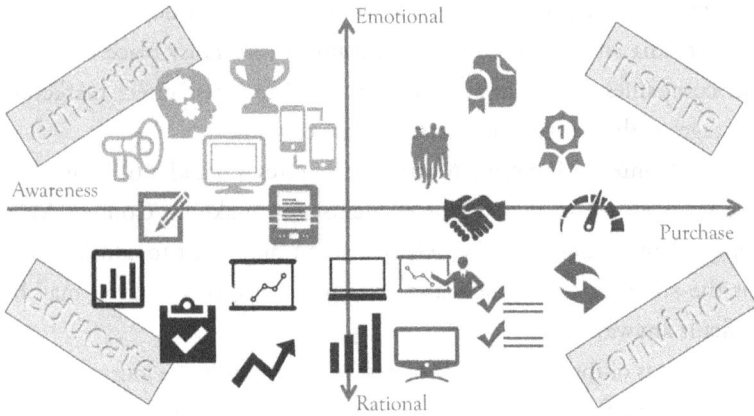

Figure 4.5 The Content Marketing Matrix

Once we have entertained our potential client, it can become difficult to keep them entertained. New and original content is often needed. We may also want to help them make the right buying decision by entertaining them with knowledge about other buyers, celebrities, reviews, and endorsements.

Not every element of the Content Marketing Matrix needs to be covered. Game-playing for a funeral company or care home might not be the right approach and for both these Entertainment may be low on the list of priorities. Similarly, interactive demos and webinars may not be required if you are selling domestic bathroom furniture.

Having a strategy for effective Content Marketing is important as the entire estate of all these elements need

	Infographics		Demo videos
	Articles		White papers
	Virals		Interactive demos
	Quizzes		Webinars
	Guides		Communities and forums
	Branded videos		Events
	Press releases		Checklists
	eBooks		Celebrity endorsements
	Competitions		Reviews and awards
	Reports		Case studies
	Games		Ratings and reviews

Figure 4.6 The Content Marketing Matrix key

to work together, and support each other in their messaging, brand identity, and style. They do not all need to look the same but there must be a logical progression from one to another, particularly where they are close neighbors on the chart as shown previously.

According to the Content Marketing Institute: *Content Marketing is a strategic marketing approach focused on creating and distributing valuable, relevant, and consistent content to attract and retain a clearly defined audience—and, ultimately, to drive profitable customer action.*

Some of the best products have failed because they were beaten by good marketing.

A great restaurant does not just need good food and a great chef, it needs good marketing and promotion, good customer reviews and referrals, and needs to provide the right atmosphere for their clientele. Even the menu style can affect what people think of the restaurant. Too busy and too much detail and it can be off-putting, not enough choice and the same result. A simple booking process or application, celebrity endorsements and interviews in the press of the chef or owner will all help. Photos of all the staff fundraising or promoting seasonal specials. All of these are elements of Content Marketing. A restaurant serving better food locally, by not doing any of the above will most likely fail by comparison.

Content Marketing must be targeted directly at the buyer. A brochure showing a house for sale must promote the house in the best way and promote the best features, whether that is the house itself, location, or local amenities. In such an example, a small starter home will have a different focus to an apartment in a retirement block.

This is not merely understanding what your customer wants but, how your customer thinks. What problem they are trying to solve, even if they do not yet know they have a problem! Using the same tone and language that your customer would use and presenting the content in a way they expect to see. A brochure for a law firm is going to be different to that for a skateboard manufacturer.

Having identified our typical customer or customers we should next focus on the type and level of information they need. How-to videos for completing a kickflip or rail-slide may be better suited to a skateboard purchaser than 20 pages of closely worded text with no graphics.

Once we know what type of content then it is a matter of matching the style to the method. If we do want to produce a podcast, then what should it be like. If we want to do live streaming then audio only or video as well? The message and the delivery mechanism are one thing but also the content and style another.

In Content Marketing, the right level of quality content matters more than everything else. It needs to be at a level that works for where the customer is in the buying journey and at a level where they want to read, not feel they must slog through to the end. A glossy brochure at the start of the buying journey will give way to something more detailed later perhaps. An endorsement video at the beginning may lead through to customer reviews and independent reports. Product sheets may lead on to white papers, and so-on.

Amidst all this we need to consider how podcasts and livestream audio works as well. While *YouTube* is the world's second largest search engine it does not mean that people get all their information from your website, glossy brochures, phone calls, and videos. Business content podcasts before 2020 were experiencing a 20 percent annual growth rate and from 2020 that accelerated again.

Podcasts are not just the mainstay of smartphones or computers. The increasing use of smart speakers in the home and, as we work more from home, as a business tool more than just a Q&A and music device, has changed how they are used. Because of its simple hands free voice activated search, it becomes easier for researchers and potential customers to ask smart speakers for a list of reviews or to listen to a podcast on a particular subject or product. The move to voice-activated search has already begun and will only accelerate and therefore, it needs to be incorporated into your Content Marketing strategy.

The most powerful part of Content Marketing is to add value. The average television viewer today often prefers to watch something later than originally broadcast. That allows the viewer to skip through adverts. Advertising slots on television or radio add little value to the viewer. Adverts may be useful as a direct promotional blunt instrument but the fact most of us skip past them demonstrates how little real value they may now actually add.

In 2014, the *Lego* Movie was released and grossed $468 million. At the same time *Lego* introduced 20 new *Lego* sets from the film. *Lego* was already a fast-growing company but, in 2014 became the world's largest toy manufacturer. How much of the sales were down to the movie and how much due to the continued growth of the company is not possible to know. However, the *Lego* Movie certainly helped, and people even paid for the privilege of watching a 1-hour 41-minute advertisement of *Lego*'s products.

Some websites are fun to watch with plenty of videos, whether it is sports, or cooking, travel, or automotive. All of them have a purpose to sell products and services and many have huge followings of people who come for the content and do not mind they are being sold to.

Adding value is not just about watching videos, or films. Giving information away for free to entice people to want to know more. Educating them and making them better informed in their buying decision, hopefully to your advantage. Providing rich content so the buyer does not need to find it elsewhere. Regular updates and newsletters so the buyers have not just the best information but also the most up to date.

Content is the foundation of almost every online customer interaction. Whether it is the initial search where they are looking for basic information, or a more detailed search. Whether the customer is searching for reviews or looking for some simple graphics to explain.

Content marketing helps a company maximize every customer interaction opportunity, at every stage in the buying process and in whatever format the buyer wants. Each element of content needs to work to get your message across as consistently and completely as the buyer would wish to consume it at that time.

Content Marketing needs to be developed strategically as a single coherent set of elements. Not an ad-hoc series of individual elements branded together to look and feel the same.

Social Selling

Leads can come at you from websites and through social media in the main. You may receive telephone calls as well as a first inquiry.

In social media, the line between leads and opportunities have been intentionally blurred. The line between what goes before—Followers and Likes—has also been blurred. Not by the social media providers but by those wishing to sell you a service to help you grow your business.

A range of companies and solo workers will promote themselves as having a lead generation system or methodology and will help you get more leads. What they are providing is a paid for service to get more followers. A follower whether a "Like" or a new connection is not a lead. A lead is a company or individual who will buy from you.

Simple product selling is a shorter process than a complex solution sale as we know, so moving from follower or connection to purchase is easier but it still needs to happen. Qualifying these connections into leads is also easier.

If you have a social media shop window or a social media site linked to a website selling something as simple as scented candles, then getting more followers or connections may indeed make them a lead. Whether they become a customer is down to what happens once you have captured their interest.

For more complex sales and in B2B, generating new followers is not a lead but gives you the opportunity to qualify them as a lead and, later potentially sell them something. For example, a sports enthusiast may "Like" *Mercedes-Benz* F1 but may be far less likely to buy a Formula 1 car. In fact, they may not own a *Mercedes-Benz* Road car or even plan to purchase one. In fact, buying a team T-shirt may also be off their list. Because those clever people in Brackley have got someone to show interest in their race team does not make me a lead to buy their products or any associated products.

For a company, being present on social media today is highly important. Being consistent in your messaging and providing a showcase to your products and services should matter on both your website and social media. However, getting more followers and connections on social media does not automatically make them a lead. No number of followers has generated a single penny of income. The only people making money from growing social media interest are those who provide the service in growing the following of others.

The more followers you do have on social media, and the more interest shown in your product and service it naturally follows that some will buy. The wider you spread your net and the more noise you make the more likely you are for some success. It also has a compounding effect. As you gather a stronger following, the dialogue between followers generates even greater visibility for your site.

You may need to moderate some of the comments, and in public forums, it can be a full-time job. However, it is important not to sanitize the conversation so much it becomes bland. Differences of opinion and opposing points of view lead to a more engaged audience and done well, allowing the positives of your product or service to rise to the top. Sometimes, allowing controversial views can win you customers but it does need careful management.

Social media can be a good source of leads and customers. It can be a great way to promote your brand and your values, and it can promote and publicize what you do. Leads can be generated from social media campaigns but not every new connection is a lead, they still need to be nurtured to buy and some will never be true sales prospects regardless of how hard you try.

To generate interest in your company or your product or service requires three things in the main, good quality and consistent content, data capture and social media visibility.

Consistency across platforms too. Accepting the restrictions of *Twitter* versus the content detail on *LinkedIn* is important to understand as too is the content style on *TikTok* versus *YouTube*. You may not want to use all of them, or they are appealing to different demographic groups. Also, you may want to experiment with one platform and not another. While the style of the message may vary, there still needs to be a coherent plan to keep them all together.

Once you have a good website and a consistent social media profile, creating clickable content on social media that generates leads or pulls people to your website should be your next objective. In terms of getting attention, social media is an incredibly busy place and getting busier all the time. You need to stand out.

Your website landing page matters. Too often companies invest in good social media content, have a well-detailed product section but the first impressions on the website lack the effort put into the other parts of marketing. The website needs to be clear, crisp, load quickly, and excite the potential buyer to want to know more.

A website landing page must be easy to read and provide users with a clear way to navigate to sign-up, or more information, or additional social content.

If a landing page involves a form, keep it simple. Each question reduces the chances of someone finishing it. The more sensitive the details, the less likely you are to get them to complete, and do you really need all that information at this stage? Pull down options or pre-filled content also helps speed up the process and improve your chance of a completed form.

According to *LinkedIn Marketing Solutions* team, their Dynamic Ad format pulls a user's name, picture, and job title across from an advert. Other tools, particularly in the job application process, pull across an entire employment history and other relevant details. According to LinkedIn, adverts that pull across just the name and job title alone gives a 19 percent higher click-through rate and 53 percent higher conversion rate than advertisements without this feature.

If the person visiting your website and form filling cannot see the reason for providing the information, they are less likely to complete it. Make sure the questions have relevance to the customers' needs.

Other techniques such as discount codes, social media contests, or exclusive content can support the process of data capture. Exclusive content can be in the form of VIP access to an event, online or otherwise, or to more detailed information, or to a more exclusive "club."

Exclusive content can be paid or free and is referred to as Gated Content. As you complete the data capture to give your potential customer access to gated content, you can also offer customers the chance to opt-in to receiving more news from your company, and immediately add them to your e-mail campaign list.

Various reports exist of the success gated content. Which works best is a mix of the type of customer you are targeting and the nature of the content you want to provide. White papers and webinars may serve business leaders better than front row seats and a chance to meet the band. Or maybe not!

Having Influencers on your side may also benefit your brand or product. However, it needs to be the right influencer in terms of their own values and their market demographic. It is not enough just to go after the one with the biggest following, especially as they are likely also to be more expensive.

Until relatively recently influencers would be seen using a product and mentioning the benefits it gave them without having to explain it was, in effect, an advertisement. Paid for content by the manufacturer to an influencer was difficult to separate from the influencer's general attitude.

In 2020, despite the UK Code of Non-broadcast Advertising and Direct & Promotional Marketing (CAP Code) and Consumer Protection Regulations (CPRs) as well as the Unfair Trading Regulations 2008, the Advertising Standards Agency and Competitions and Markets Authority felt it necessary to make it clear what were the rules for influencers and product promotion. The law did not change but the increasing presence and impact of influencers meant the regulators felt it sufficiently necessary to make clear the rules.

In some markets and for some products, influencer marketing can reach a bigger audience of targeted prospects quicker than many other methods. It allows you to "borrow" an influencer's audience and get them to promote your brand. It is also highly targeted.

One thing to remember, not all influencers are A-list celebrities. Having Roger Federer, Thierry Henry, and Tiger Woods promote *Gillette* razor blades or a George Clooney promoting a *Nespresso* coffee maker may not be for everyone. Influencers may have local or regional influence or specific demographics.

Choosing the right influencer can have a significant impact on your brand, for good or for bad, it may lead to increased sales but nothing is a guarantee. In 2016, Ariana Renee, an *Instagram* influencer, with over two million followers created her own T-shirt brand. She had to sell a small number of T-shirts from the first run for the printer to produce more. She failed to hit her first target and sold less than the 36 required. Not all "influencers" actually wield influence.

All leads generated through social media need to be analyzed. Various tools, many free, exist to capture data, so you can see what is working through various channels and what types of campaigns and adverts work best. Known as Social Analytics, these tools also allow you to identify the type of creative and messaging that performs best. Taking that data and producing from it the insight that allows you to tune and improve is critical in the success of social media campaign development.

Having the best written and most informative content may not generate significant interest. Having the best product might, but there are many examples of products that are less than ideal becoming incredibly successful, mainly down to how they achieved social media visibility. Similarly, some great products failed because they did not win over the customers, or the businesses required to make them a success.

Online Reviews were originally the mainstay of social spending, holidays, restaurants, places to visit, and so on. It is now much more common for the reviews to be for all products and services and, very often, the review is more about the customer service, the promptness and simplicity rather than the product at all. However, in large B2B deals online reviews do not always readily apply.

Reviewing comments others have made on their experiences tends to happen early in the buying process. Customers are hardly likely to read a restaurant review when they are already seated at a table. That poses a challenge for the supplier. If a small batch of recent reviews are negative, it becomes a challenge to entice people in to demonstrate the improvements made and return to more favorable reviews.

The other challenge for companies with reviews in the public domain is readers will often look for the lowest ratings rather than the best.

Resetting the bias in favor is possible. Fake reviews and influencer reviews can all help but the companies that provide reviewed data have tools and systems to monitor both the reviewers and the reviewed to spot anomalies or sudden changes in patterns and trends.

For some industries, online reviews are far more important than advertising. When looking at a retirement home for example.

Keeping track of reviews on specialist online review sites and other social media sites can be a large task. However, solutions exist to capture all the relevant review data into a database and analyze it. Some tools even provide an interface to allow the supplier to respond to comments through the information capture application rather than visiting each different website.

Tools used to track multiple review sites can capture all these data and give even greater insight into the type of customer. Identifying the demographics of the biggest complainers versus the biggest supporters or what products have a better score in certain outlets or geographies can all provide useful insight to a company.

It is worth mentioning here that even chatbots can influence your potential customer. A simple inquiry can be dealt with easily and efficiently or can be made difficult depending on how much resource you commit to chatbots. There are Fintechs that have no call centers, that have instead invested heavily in chatbots backed up by real people. What makes their chatbot effective is that it has multiple answers for the same question, just a slight variation on the wording. It also has shorthand, text-speak, and spelling mistakes. The perception for the user is they are messaging with a real person. Despite all the technological advancements and the fact that we accept chatbots, we still like to believe we are exchanging messages with a real person.

Buying Leads

Temptation is often to buy a list as it fills the top of the funnel quickly. Despite the fact lists can be bought that are highly defined based on many parameters, it still poses a challenge in finding the real opportunities among all that initial data.

Buying leads is often a lot less expensive than generating leads through campaigns but there are hurdles from the start. Even if the lead has opted in to receive information from third parties, and we sincerely hope you would not use any other type. They still require nurturing, they require educating, and we still do not know if they are at the right stage in the buying cycle or even have a genuine need.

Whether you are using a list to e-mail companies, or perhaps text message them, or whether the approach is to cold call them, they are still not expecting you to contact them and are likely unaware of who you are, certainly not to any great depth.

Sending e-mails that will get read is challenging. Calling someone unannounced is likely to interrupt their day. However, the two combined with the right e-mail title and some advanced information pre-empting a call is perhaps the best approach for larger opportunities. For large volume, sales perhaps pick both but run them as separate campaigns to see what is most effective.

Buying lists may count against you and turn your e-mail into Spam. That is even if the recipient accepted, they wanted to add their details to a list. Once you are on one spam list, it is likely Internet Service Providers (ISPs) will share that with each other and you soon join a growing list of identified spammers.

Old and redundant e-mail addresses are likely to hit your ratings. Hard-bounces of about 5 percent or more of your e-mails will flag you to the ISPs and will affect your e-mail-sending reputation. It is important, therefore, to keep your e-mail list current and clean and make sure all opt-outs and those not opted in are removed from your lists.

ISPs also look for key words and phrases in the subject line of e-mails, to alert that you may be a potential spammer. Anything that sounds overtly like a promotion or a trigger to action is likely to cause an issue. Avoid "free" or "guarantee" or "just for you" and similar phrases in the e-mail title wherever you can. Tools exist for you to input the body of your e-mail and the titles and for it to be scored or validated for how likely it is to get picked up by spam filters.

Spam filters exist not only at the ISP but also on company servers and can block files with some types of attachments. Though that may not always be the case it may be better to refer the prospective client to a part of your website that has the information or to a research document that reinforces your point.

You must include a simple and easy to use unsubscribe button or link and a physical address in your e-mail footer.

Allowing people the option to unsubscribe is not only important in terms of keeping a clean sheet with ISPs, it is also a legal requirement. Although most recipients' preference is to keep it simple, often we see companies redirecting the reader to a webpage where a series of questions are asked, or the recipient is asked to opt out of different types of e-mail. One of the worst examples of this is, ironically enough, a well-known e-mail marketing platform!

It is easy to get on a list of identified spammers and much harder to get off it. Over time, a concerted effort to clean up your act will help but it does take time. However, there are tools to help, you can get a score of your online performance as regards spam and take corrective action to improve it.

In the same way that you can be marked out as a Spammer, cold calling people without permission and generating complaints as a result, can also impact your ability to connect with prospective clients. Often referred to as Nuisance Calls or Nuisance Messages.

Fixed line and mobile phone companies keep a list of complaints and nuisance callers. Once a call center or agency or an individual has been identified, by recipients registering a complaint, nuisance calls are flagged to a mobile or barred from a landline, if the recipient has opted into fixed line call barring. Different countries have different approaches for managing fixed line nuisance calls.

Competitive Analysis

Sales pursuits do not sit in isolation. They need to be considered against other pursuits and which ones you should, therefore, commit to doing. They should also be assessed against the competitive offerings such that pursuits where the competition is much stronger than you or has a much better fit, are quickly dismissed.

No player or team in the professional era of any sport goes out not knowing what the opponent(s) have in their arsenal and what their game plan will be. In 1974, George Foreman fought Muhammed Ali in a world heavyweight boxing match. Foreman was the current champion; Ali previously being stripped of all his titles. Foreman was getting odds of 4 to 1 to win. Leading up to the fight, Ali went out of his way to rile Foreman, the latter generally regarded as being the stronger hitter. The fight was known for Ali's rope-a-dope approach where he spent the entire opening rounds leaning on the ropes and letting Foreman work him over. Brutal though it was Foreman could not break Ali down who soaked up the onslaught. From the fourth round, Foreman was tiring and the strategy Ali had adopted seemed to be working. The fight ended in the eighth round but was won months before when Ali changed his training program, got the right team around him, developed the tactics to win and started to position his competition where he wanted them.

To understand the competitive landscape several tools are available. The most widely known and perhaps easiest to use tool is SWOT— Strengths, Weaknesses, Opportunities, Threats.

Not every company needs to undertake a competitive analysis and you do not need to analyze all your competitors or review this at every pursuit. However, competitive analysis does not need to be an ongoing and consistent process but, if you do undertake competitive analysis, it makes sense to periodically check and update, especially when major events happen in the industry, the marketplace or with one of your competitors, or indeed your own company.

Some salespeople are keen to dismiss competitive analysis crib-sheets either because they believed they knew everything about their competitor already or because they felt it not relevant to their role, it was seen more as a marketing function to know the competitors. There is some truth in that, salespeople should be focused on selling their solution, not on the competitors. But, to play to your strengths means also know the competitors' weaknesses.

Competitor crib-sheets are good tools to use. Often, we see coaches on the side-lines with sheets of paper. We naturally think it is notes for their team, but often it contains notes about the competitor team.

As well as directing your sales message, competitor crib-sheets help salespeople understand what they will promote as their best suit. It allows you to channel your efforts in directing your client to the areas where your biggest competitor is weakest. Sometimes it is not just about playing to your strengths, it is about playing up against their weaknesses.

Not all competitors sell directly, some may have resellers and partner channels. A reseller may have several competing products they are selling so understanding which one they will go with may be difficult and, in the early stages it may not be apparent even to them. Understanding also who they partner with versus who you partner with matters if it is a complex sale involving critical third parties.

There is a significant amount to understand about competitive analysis, not least of which is that it begins with understanding the customer. Developing customer personas, or avatars, is the first stage. However, as we are concerned with sales in this book, let us focus on what competitive analysis offers the sales pursuit.

When in the sales pursuit, it matters that we know the competition, who they are, what is their approach, how well they are progressing.

Often this is hard to ascertain but simply asking the potential customer can provide surprising results. If that does not work, try business social media, such as LinkedIn and see who from your target client and your competitors are now connected. Check the visitors log at reception when visiting your client.

If you know your contact is conducting a series of meetings back-to-back, turn up 20 minutes early, apologies that your earlier meeting finished on time and there was no traffic. Work from reception on your laptop. See who leaves while you are waiting. Remember, on the way out, you may get the same treatment so make sure you have a fantastic sign-off and good rapport as you do, standing in reception, your competitor may be watching.

Check out the cars in the car park. Not everyone drives a sign-written panel van and, perhaps, taking photographs of vehicle registration plates may be a little extreme. There may be clues from the cars parked in the visitors' bays such as brochures or a car that looks familiar from a previous opportunity. Having left the building, get in the car, and spend the next 10 minutes making calls and see who arrives to park their car or walks across to the building entrance.

No professional sports team would ever enter the arena without coaches advising them, having spent hours watching videos and reading endless amounts of statistical analysis. In many respects, this has spoiled professional sport. The opportunity for individuality and instant creative brilliance is gone. Now, there are no surprises, and you already know what the opposition will do and how they will play, long before you start getting changed.

Marketing Is the First Stage in Sales

Marketing is set as a separate department from Sales and very often has a different head of department, certainly in larger companies. But, with the advent of role titles such as Chief Revenue Officer (CRO), the two are beginning to share a common form in some organizations. Sometimes seen as competitive rather than complimentary, Marketing and Sales should work together to form what is the first part of the Sales Funnel.

Old model   New model

Marketing

Awareness

Interest

Consideration

Evaluation

Decision

Sales

Purchase

Repeat

Loyality

Advocacy

Marketing

Sales

Marketing

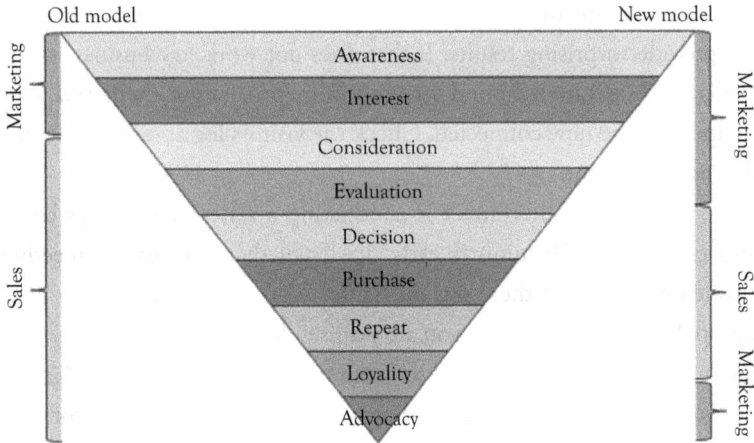

Figure 4.7 The changing influence between Marketing and Sales

Depending on how your organization is structured and the complexity of the solution marketing may reach farther into and further down the Sales Funnel.

Traditionally, marketing used to be focused on raising awareness and stimulating interest for the sales teams to engage with unqualified leads and turn them into prospects. This is now just as likely to be done within the marketing team in some organizations.

The Sales Funnel is an oversimplification of the entire process and takes no account for any of the complex processes the buyer may go through or that the seller is required to perform. It is also linear and does not allow for upsell, cross-sell, or change of plans. However, it does offer both sides—customer and seller—a simple process to follow.

In some organizations, it is now for marketing to consider if it wants to continue with a sales opportunity at the early stages. Taking the decision away from the sales team that hold the target are more directly compensated as a result could offer a more pragmatic view or, as mathematical statistician Nassim Nicholas Taleb states: *"When I don't have skin in the game, I am usually dumb."*

In some organizations, marketing goes even beyond that, offering the prospective customer more than the qualification stages and engaging in open dialogue about their needs, their intent to buy, and the process the client is to follow. This has the advantage that the sales team get hard-qualified leads to close but, as a customer, it does take a little getting used to.

The marketing team, potentially with telesales now included, has spent time building a good rapport with the prospect and worked hard at qualifying them and getting a good understanding of their needs. Now that must be handed over to a salesperson to close out the remainder of the process and win the deal. Aside from the fact, the prospect may feel he has a good relationship—people buy from people—and now that changes late in the process, no matter how efficient the process, there will always be something missed in the handover.

For an almost exclusively online process where the last stage is perhaps a video call or a meeting then this process can be effective and does offer an efficient way to win business. However, for other solution sales or for building a lasting client relationship, it may not offer the best approach.

There are no rules on where you draw the line between Marketing and Sales, indeed perhaps there is no line as such, more a blurring in the middle. However, that these two integral parts work together efficiently to deliver the best results is vital to the success of sales. Salespeople should be actively interested in what Marketing is doing.

> One of the best Marketing people I ever worked with shared a desk directly opposite me. We worked well together and shared ideas from our respective desks to work well as a team. From my experience, most companies could do with more collaboration and better team working between Marketing and Sales.

Key Takeaways

The Marketing Mix is where all Marketing begins. It provides an effective structure to all the elements related to the product or service. It allows the supplier to evaluate their product against the competition and against what the market needs. It also helps the company more broadly understand what efforts and changes it needs to make in order to be more successful.

I would argue Plant and Partnership are now sufficiently important that they deserve a seat at the table and the 9 Ps should be the norm for any Marketing Mix.

How the Marketing Mix elements are perceived by the company selling and how they are seen by the client may vary and the resulting gap analysis provide useful insight into product development, staff training, pricing, and much more besides.

Simply understanding the Marketing Mix and being able to compare is not an output. Having better understanding is not, of itself, something to win more business. To do that requires a lot more.

Digital Marketing is a term that goes back to the 1990s. In 1993, the first clickable banner went live online. Today we take for granted the amount of online content. However, not all online marketing appeals to all buyers and not all online marketing serves the same requirements for the reader/viewer/listener or for the marketing department.

Online marketing needs to provide a range from simple soundbites and images through to detailed content and facts. It needs to educate and entertain, and it needs to excite and win over the hearts and the minds of the buyer. The Marketing department in any large business needs to field players with a range of skills to move the ball from one end to the other and score the winning goal. The Content Marketing Matrix is the field of play and each element is one of the team of players. They may not all be on the field at the same time, but they need to be there when needed.

The Content used and deployed by Marketing needs to reflect the customer needs and the competitive landscape. It needs to drive the start of the sales pursuit and stimulate the first shoots of interest. But Marketing is no longer a one department task. As with Sales, Marketing too is now a team sport. Social selling means everyone in a business can have a social media account and promote their company's products. Similarly, their personal profile can be used to underpin or undermine the values of the very company that employs them.

Social selling can be a huge undertaking for some companies, particularly in the business to consumer world of high demand products and services. As a result of this high profile, it requires close management and not just in-house. Employees, past–employees, and disgruntled customers can all be an issue on social media. However, done well social media can become a sales tool and have a major impact too.

Keeping customers happy and engaged is now so important to companies that the task of looking after customers postsale and during or post implementation is no longer left just to the implementation team of the Account Manager. Marketing is now required to directly engage and work with happy and disgruntled customers alike. To turn challenges into opportunities and to turn positive feedback into marketing messages.

CHAPTER 5

Customer Satisfaction

Overview

Accepting the cost of retaining a customer is less than the cost of acquiring a new one or that the opportunity to upsell and cross-sell to existing customers adds value then it follows that making sure customers are satisfied is important. However, the odds are stacked against the supplier purely by the virtue of human nature. So, satisfying a customer is not enough, we must delight our customers rather than just make sure they got what they paid for.

Customer Satisfaction is the measure of how well we are doing as suppliers. Delight a customer and they will possibly recommend you to someone else. But underperform and customers, whether individual or corporate, will be much more likely to complain.

Simply being a provider that gives the customer what they want, timely, efficiently, and at a decent price may get some positive endorsements but that is no guarantee. That does not mean you should not measure, however. Measuring Customer Satisfaction is not about enticing an endorsement out of them, it is about understanding today where we are valued and for tomorrow to make the changes and improvements needed.

Customer Satisfaction is now so important that companies specialize in helping our customer score and measure and putting into place actions to improve. Some companies may even list their Customer-Sat score on their website as a badge of honor for how well they are doing.

There are, in effect, three ways to measure Customer Satisfaction. All provide a different perspective of the customer experience and the relationship they have with their supplier.

The Customer Needs to Be Satisfied

Whether the job title is Customer Champion or Head of Customer Excellence matter nought, it is the attitude and belief in getting everything right for the customer that matters. But there is a narrow line between being a champion of the customer and going into bat on behalf of the customer.

In the same way that everyone is in sales, but we may not all be salespeople, it is true to say that everyone in an organization has some responsibility for ensuring customers are happy, or at the very least, content.

Customer Satisfaction is a measure of how satisfied a customer is with the products and services you offer and the support and advice they receive from you. It is not Customer Service though that does play a part in the race to satisfy your customers.

In a paper entitled "A Theory of Human Behaviour" in 1943, Abraham Maslow delivered his Hierarchy of Needs, see Figure 5.1 below. Today this is one of the most widely recognizable charts. However, applying it to business is something rarely done but is something that should be done to understand the customer.

We think of the Hierarchy of Needs in personal terms in general life terms. We need a place to live, food, shelter, warmth, and so on. We need

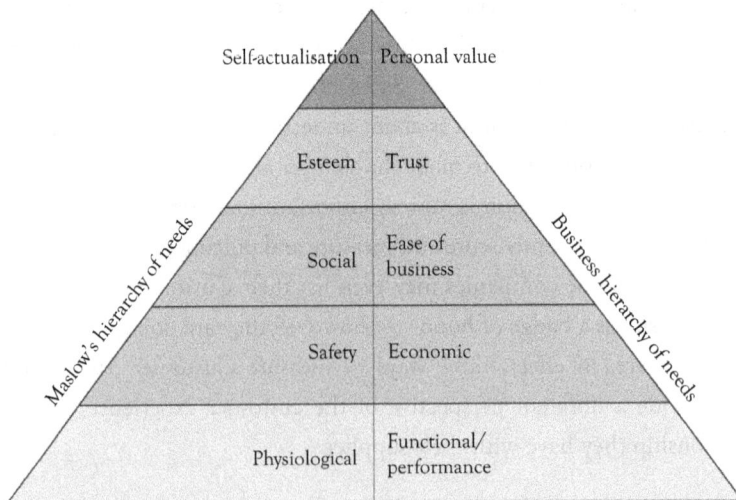

Figure 5.1 Maslow's Hierarchy of Needs in the business environment

social interaction. The very fact that sits firmly in the middle of our needs pyramid is demonstrated best by what happened in 2020 and 2021.

Starting in late 2019, a virus spread around the world causing a huge upheaval to society. The pandemic that followed wrapped itself around the globe had a huge impact on rich and poor alike, countries and people. Drastic measures were introduced in many advanced economies where the complex interaction of society was driving infection rates ever higher.

The full fallout of working from home and homes-schooling has yet to be seen but most people have suffered in isolation to a greater or lesser degree. But it is not the family group isolation that is the issue, it is the lack of "what else."

> I have worked from home since 1994. I remember explaining it many times to my friends how it worked, and how many of them did not truly get the concept. Indeed, my partner would telephone me throughout the day to ask if I had done all manner of chores and tasks; I think she understood the "home" bit better than the "working" bit. Today, however, working from home is not so uncommon.

The isolationism is not the working from home, it is the lack of socializing, whether with colleagues in an office or friends over dinner. It is the lack of belonging; window shopping, listening to other people's conversations on the train or in the coffee shop, the noise and hubbub of social society, of being able to socially integrate with others.

Maslow's Hierarchy of Needs can, and should, be applied in business as well as to us all individually. In truth, there are two ways the Hierarchy of Needs can be applied in a business, the first for the customer and the second for the business itself.

Physiological Needs. We need the product to work, we need it to do what it is designed to do. We need it to fulfill a purpose for us. If we are buying vitamins, we need to know what the pill will give us in pure numbers form. Very few of us will know enough about our body's needs to fully understand all this stuff so we take it as read and we hear advice from respected people—doctors, dieticians, and so on. We then simply apply what we have been told to what it says on the packet.

Other products may have a more directly involved process for deciding if it fits our basic needs. We are thirsty and walk into a shop. Do we buy a bottle of water or do we buy a packet of crisps (chips for my American friends and colleagues). The answer is simple of course but one of these will satisfy the physiological need, the other not. Even if we are hungry as well.

Customer Satisfaction is making sure every bottle of water tastes good, the supply chain delivers enough to the shop and customers get what they want. In the packet of crisps, the "chips" are fresh and not crushed down to a pulp.

Safety Needs reflect the impact the supplier or product has on us in other ways. Vegetarians baulk at eating meat of course, and in the Hierarchy of Needs this sits in their Safety Needs requirement. Beyond lifestyle choices, we can consider our environmental leanings perhaps. However, most of our decision-buying criteria is simpler; in B2C, it would be the price or value for money and B2B perhaps also the Return on Investment (RoI).

Where Customer Satisfaction is most prominent in a business is in the space marked Social Interaction. The ease of doing business, the process for handling complaints, the ability to correct mistakes.

Modern society requires Social Interaction to take place across multiple platforms, indeed often in a nonsocial way! Whether it is social media, chatbots, messaging, e-mails, or call centers; how we interact with our customers matters. It matters how many channels and how well. It is simply not enough to show up online, have a portal, and think that is enough.

I was at the checkout of a shop, buying some hardware. The young woman at the till clearly did not want to be there and her manner with the people in front was obvious. If she could have thrown everything harder and farther down the conveyor belt she would. No eye contact, nothing but the merest of grunts in between the occasional begrudging word.

Not to be defeated, I tried to lift her mood. Every item that she picked, scanned, and tossed items in my general direction it was met with a cheery *"thank you"* from me. Nothing. No change, no reaction at all from the young woman serving. I persisted and, after paying, in cash, and accepting my change I reached for my final attempt in customer relationship management.

"Excuse me, I have been very polite. It would be nice if you said thank you."

The checkout assistant responded, "Don't have to, it says so on the receipt."

Social Needs are not just about the customer, they apply equally to the staff, the team, the workers. In the aforementioned example they clearly impact the customer experience, although I do begrudgingly admire the fact that in this particular social swordfight she won.

How you look after your employees and fellow workers directly impacts the relationship you have with your customers. The adage that "the Customer is always right" needs to sit shoulder to shoulder with:

Employees come first. If you take care of your employees, they will take care of the clients.

—Richard Branson

In the world of business, Social Needs are really all about how easy it is to do business, how enjoyable the experience is and how likely you are, as a result, to return.

If you have ever bought a low-cost airline ticket then tried to get a refund or make a change you will know that it is not an easy task. The buying experience up front is super slick and efficient. For most customers this, and the price, is all that matters. So, if the complaints process is tortuous then perhaps, they do not want you as a customer and they will stick with the 90 percent that do not make a fuss.

Ease of doing business does not apply to everyone and does not apply at every stage, where it matters most is determined by the type of customer you want and how much effort you wish to make to the outliers in your target market.

Thanks to the Fourth Industrial Revolution, ease of doing business has improved significantly. Known also as Industry 4.0, it is the automation of industry, using machine-to-machine communication, and the Internet of Things (IoT). Integrated for increased automation, improved communication, and self-monitoring, to analyze and manage without the need for human intervention.

Take something we consider today as simple as opening a bank account. Install the App, upload some information, scan a few documents, and all you must wait for now is a piece of plastic to arrive in the post. In fact, you may not even want the card. Today opening a business bank account should take less than 10 minutes.

Compare that with how people opened my first bank account even as recently as 10 years ago. Customers had to make an appointment with the bank and come armed with all manner of identification information, proof of address, income statements, and so on. Lots of form filling, multiple versions of my signature to be stored on different systems.

If we now apply the technology alone to the original process, it would not make it any quicker or easier. Accepted background checks would be quicker and making an appointment and the signature may now be on a tablet not paper. What has changed is the processes have been optimized using the technology to make the experience better. Technology alone will not improve the ease of doing business.

Some people have greater Esteem Needs than others. In the world of business, it follows that some companies, and some industries, have a greater degree of trustworthiness. You perhaps trust your dentist more than you do your dry cleaner!

For Customer Satisfaction, **Esteem** manifests itself in quite a different way. As customer loyalty increases so customers look for some recognition, they look to be rewarded. In many cases additional discounts, invitation to special events, part of an "inner circle," early notice of new product lines. These are all good marketing tools and will build desire in those not at that level and improve loyalty for those that reach it. But it is also about Esteem.

Social Media has heightened the need for many people in society to want greater recognition. As somebody once put it, social media is about "buying things you don't need, with money you don't have, to impress people you don't know."

We are all guilty of showcasing our own, special experience. Whether it is to build self-esteem, or to "show off" to others matters naught to the company selling, if the word gets out there.

As people want greater recognition, companies can turn this to their advantage, not just for loyalty purposes, but also for social media marketing through their own customers.

Customers see they are valued more highly. Customers become even more loyal. Customer shares the success reward with his peer group and on social media. Customer becomes an advocate for your brand/product. More customers arrive.

Customer Satisfaction can be delivered through attention to Customer Needs.

The trouble with Maslow's Hierarchy of Needs is twofold. First, it is not a hierarchy. Accepted there is some logic behind the way the layers are built up, but it does not follow that one leads to another or that one should be completed/achieved before moving onto the next.

But are they all needed? In the world generally perhaps not. In the world of business certainly not. We may aspire to high esteem, but I doubt it is an actual need.

In Maslow's Hierarchy of Needs, **Self-Actualization** is simply that you have achieved the very pinnacle of what you can be. In the world of Customer Satisfaction perhaps we should rename this Supercustomer Actualization.

Maslow's Hierarchy of Needs does not apply to a modern world. For example, Ozan Dağdeviren in his book *Ait* states:

> *Perhaps, Maslow, who set up this model, would not realize the self-realization of the pyramid if it had grown up in a collective society such as India, rather than in a society like America, which adopted a strongly Accurate style .... It is time to leave behind Maslow's flat, hierarchical and life-simplistic system: with a dynamic system based*

on interaction, giving space to complexity, in which needs are not
parallel and can be met independently

The best example of Supercustomer Actualization is a well-known department store. Their top customers, through spend and loyalty, get personal shoppers, have a dedicated suite of rooms to use when they visit where clothes and other items are brought to them. Food and drinks are laid on, everything is packed, wrapped, and delivered to the customer's home the same day. The store will even arrange this out of hours and has a dedicated private entrance to the room at the top of the building for the experience. The same department store will also send you birthday cards, occasional gifts, invitations to super-VIP events, and exclusive offers. This may be as close to Self-Actualization that we can get for a customer.

Measuring Customer Satisfaction

It is wrong to suppose that if you can't measure it, you can't manage
it—a costly myth

—W. Edwards Deming

There are several ways to generate a score from customers and several ways you can score Customer Satisfaction. The length of time you have a customer and the number of products they buy will impact the score they give you as will their peers and even people they do not know. What is clear, however, is that Customer Satisfaction matters for long-term relationships and in a B2B environment it is the personal score of individuals as much as the collective score of the company that matters.

Survey tools, be that online or directly by phone or face to face, can be used to collect customer feedback. Asking a single question or multiple questions will get you the data but too many questions or too complex questions and you may not get the answer you want or the number of completed surveys may not be the number you need. Keep it simple and keep it short.

We are today swamped with online surveys. That poses a problem. The customer is not as engaged as you would like, and you now must "earn the right" to ask the questions. Companies sometimes resort to incentives to get surveys completed but how engaged the responder is when they are there because of the carrot not because of their experience remains open for debate.

Web-forms are often used as survey questionnaires and are a short-form version perhaps focused on one element. Through 2020, we were all constantly being asked by multiple video-conferencing companies about our experience as we left a web-call. In truth, the question was completely irrelevant to what they were doing but it made us feel our feedback mattered! If there was ever likely to be an issue with the call it would be bandwidth not application related, something they had no control over.

Some industry sectors have taken to mobile messaging surveys. Several online banks and multiple delivery companies that do this. The assumption from these companies is that you transact through an App. So, therefore, you will be willing to complete a survey the same way. None of these, widely or generally publish statistics on the number of fully completed surveys. It is, therefore, likely to be an extremely low response rate.

Live chat online may be a good tool to capture feedback from customers. If done through the course of helping them with an issue it feels less invasive. If done at the end when the attendant asks if you would not mind completing a survey based on your experience, then the drop off is, not surprisingly, extremely high.

Live chat may take more time than surveys which can be fully automated but for large organizations investment in Artificial Intelligence (AI) can help reduce some of the manual work. Many Live-chat attendants are fully AI today, complete with shorthand response and intentional spelling errors, to make you believe you are in fact text messaging a real person.

Direct communication with customers, by telephone or in person, and by e-mail can also capture feedback. Simply asking a customer on a call what they thought of a product or, for bigger clients, what they would like to see changed about the products or how you support them can be a good way to measure not just satisfaction but their long-term needs and just how well you are doing today versus their expectations for the future.

Do be careful when asking clients what they want from the future relationship or product. You might get set targets you cannot achieve. What began as a casual conversation may later become a stick to beat you with or a product want becomes a product need and you find yourself falling short. That is not to say, do not have the conversation, but use this with caution and not with every client.

Where Channel Partners are involved, it may be difficult to get direct customer feedback. It may also not be in the Channel Partner's best interest to pass on all the feedback either because it reflects badly on them or because it gives data to their competitors.

Online, analysis of customer shopping and browsing patterns, webpage visits and downloads as well as other data can help provide information about your clients. Your website may have data analytics tools built in to help generate insights and reports.

In the direct retail world, best practice is the one last question approach. It may seem a little blunt instrument but that does not make it less valuable. Just asking the right question at the end of the buying process to get a soft metric can be useful. Done well, just asking the question can leave a positive impression with the customer.

Not every company cares for face-to-face feedback. "Do you want fries with that" cares nothing for customer satisfaction and all for cross/upselling. Followed by "Have a nice day" again no interest in the customer's experience more an instruction to go away.

Asking the one question in face-to-face retail it also matters that tone, intent, and body language are all correct.

Think about the last restaurant you went to. At some point the waiter will ask something like "Everything okay with your meal?" How many times have you been mid-conversation or have a mouth full of food when asked? Has the waiter stopped to wait for you to respond or, better still, waited until you are ready for a short conversation?

Often it may be done as a walk-by on the way to another table. If there was a problem with the meal, the diner should have already made it known to the waiter rather than carry-on regardless. Yet we all put up with this and it does nothing to improve customer satisfaction, potentially it is just annoying.

The prestigious Royal *Automobile Club in London's* Pall Mall houses one of my favourite restaurants. The *RAC* provides great food and a relaxed atmosphere in a wonderful building, but it is perhaps the way they treat customers that makes it different. How they attend to Customer Satisfaction is through good Customer Service.

A waiter will always make sure the water is topped up, without asking, and wine glasses filled. All without the slightest hint of fuss or interruption. Only when he or she notices I have stopped eating and there is a lull in the conversation will he or she ask. The question is often thoughtful and informative and shows care for the customer. Rather than the typical *how is your lunch?* without the waiter so much as breaking stride that you get from most restaurants, the waiter here is more likely to be *I'm glad you went for the Sea Bass. The sauce is something new from the Chef, it would be good to tell him what you think.*

This is not an invasive question. It takes little time to respond but requires me to think and therefore engage in the conversation and give useful feedback as well as the impression that my views count.

In the example above, yes, there is a lot of blurring between Customer Service and Customer satisfaction. However, the question is done to get feedback but also to get a response from me that lets them know how well they are doing and how satisfied I am by the overall experience. Even if the food was great and there was an issue with something else it is an open question and allows me to raise another matter should I wish to.

Scoring Customer Satisfaction

Customer Satisfaction can be scored in several ways, such as CES, CSAT, and NPS. Collectively, we may often refer to these as Customer Experience (CX).

The Customer Effort Score (CES) is a measure of how easy, or difficult, it is to do business. It can be applied online or in person and can be a question you put to the customer at various times, such as point of order, dealing with returns, handling complaints, and so on.

There are two statistics that explain what CES is important. In a report published by *Harvard Business Review* in 2010: *94% of consumers who report their interactions with a brand being 'low effort' will repurchase.* And, according to an article by *Hubspot: 91% of customers reporting high effort saying they would speak negatively about the company to others.*

CES should be done immediately after the interaction. The customer is more likely to respond at that time and the accuracy of their response will be better. But, as with any survey, keeping it short and simple and not asking the customer to spend too much time on this is key. Often, just one question is enough.

Unlike CES which scores the ease of doing business the Customer Satisfaction Score (CSAT) is a more general measure, used to measure how positive, or negative, a customer's experience has been. CSAT is calculated from customer responses to a simple grading question or set of simple questions, very often online.

We see CSAT surveys today at places of high consumer traffic where touch buttons are installed for immediate customer reaction, such as an airport arrivals hall, or public lavatories. The obvious questions: who touched the button before?

In most instances, it is a simple one-rating system ranging between very good/positive to very poor/unsatisfactory. Online there is the opportunity to have several simple rating scores that people are asked to do, but you should always begin with a general statement on the overall experience.

Combining the scores from a CSAT survey is a matter of seeing how many rated their experience at each of the levels. Multichannel companies can compare one channel with another to learn about the customer experience and make changes. Different regions and territories may even react differently with different expectations.

CSAT can be done multiple times through the process. In long and complex sales and ongoing customer relationships, this may help you spot trends in customer loyalty and where you need to make improvements in the process.

CSAT is also an effective way of measuring the success of a change to a product or the buying process with your customers.

CSAT does have some disadvantages. Studies have shown that we tend to vote more toward the extremes in these kinds of surveys. The preference is either very positive or very negative rather than mildly so or neutral. It also brings with it consumer prejudices. There may be nothing wrong with the queue at the airport security check-in but if the person in front of you was totally disorganized, had to go multiple times through the metal detector, and had unacceptable items in their baggage you may score the process down, regardless of the fact the issue was not within the control of Border Control.

CSATs are best done immediately after purchase or, if it is a long process, at key stages in the buying process. But too much and the CSAT scoring process will facilitate lower scores.

Customers who must renew a product or services, perhaps annually, are also worth surveying. How often and how detailed is up to you but perhaps no more than every six months for something like an annual membership subscription. Not only does this let you know whether the customer is still using, and still valuing, your service, but it also gives you the opportunity to inform the customer you care about what they think. Often it can be a prompt for a follow-up call or for them to call you.

CSATs can be undertaken seasonally, to fit in with customer buying cycles or other products, competitors and complimentary, or to engage with them outside of the normal buying cycle or process.

For companies with large numbers of customers deploying CSAT gives a rolling review of the company's performance and the value of its services and products. Making a change and watching the scores change, or not, can give early insight to things you have changed for the better or things that customers do not like.

Big companies and small alike can make costly mistakes but thinking they know better and not testing first. In 1985, *Coca Cola* introduced "New Coke" changing the formula that had been for 100 years. The arguments made sense; it was sweeter than before using corn syrup. What can go wrong with making a sweet drink even sweeter?

Coca Cola knew from the start it was a bold move and set up a way for customers to give feedback. It blew up in spectacular fashion; at one point, only 18 percent of consumers rated the new coke better than the old. *Pepsi*, their biggest rival, went to town on an advertising campaign and in some U.S. states, there were helplines for people to call and complain. In one U.S. state, there was a petition to the company to change the recipe back.

New Coke lasted 77 days before the company faced the press and confessed to having made a mistake. The irony of all this is it generated a lot of post event publicity and saw a surge in sales and improved their leader over rival *Pepsi Cola*.

If you think *Pepsi* always gets it right; in 1989, *Pepsi* introduced a high-caffeine version of its drink called *Pepsi A.M.* It was only piloted in some U.S. states and failed to catch on so was quickly pulled.

In both cases, *Coca Cola* and *Pepsi Cola*, customer feedback was vital in the decisions the company made. For *Coke*, however, they thought they knew better whereas *Pepsi* experimented first. Using CSAT will give you the information you need but there are perhaps better ways of experimenting with your products or services than a Hail Mary Pass approach.

CSAT has the advantage that it is short to do and offers a simple rating scale. Therefore, it typically gets a high response rate. However, it is open to cultural bias which vary not just from country to country but even region and other cultural differences. Differences in how women and men score and even the time of day that a score is taken can all have an impact.

Customers completing CSAT surveys tend to score in the extremes. Those who feel very passionate for or against their experience are more likely to give a score than those in the middle ranges. That it is a snapshot in time does not always reflect well in ongoing Customer Satisfaction.

The survey term "satisfied" is about as vanilla as one can get. It is a relatively neutral word, rather than perhaps something like excited, delighted, or even delicious. To understand how a customer feels about your product or service, or company, instead of ranking their assessment it may be better to ask them a more engaging set of questions.

Net Promotor Scores (NPS) helps measure customer satisfaction by asking them if they are likely to recommend your product or service to a friend. In fact, you can begin a survey with a CSAT question first and then continue with NPS-based questions.

NPS was developed by Fred Reichheld of Bain and Company in 2003 and is universally used by companies around the world. However, for most companies using NPS they tend to use the scoring methodology and not the other elements of NPS which involve a process of learning and improvement. In short, companies use the scoring method as a start but do not always follow the full methodology.

Customer referrals begin from within. If you cannot get the people who work for a company to recommend it first, then asking customers to do so will be a greater challenge. According to Fred Reichheld:

> *Many executives …, want the economic advantages of customer loyalty but ignore the inspirational side of NPS. They forget that it's impossible to create loyal customers without first inspiring a team of employees, so they become promoters themselves.*

Like all good Customer Satisfaction measures, NPS is easy to use and, therefore, gets a lot of customer feedback. Unlike CES and CPS, however, it is an indicator of future growth as well as current performance, the other two only focusing on the current only.

The methodology is simple. You ask the customer how likely they are to recommend the product or service, or your company, to a friend on a rating 1 to 10 (or 1 to 100), see Figures 5.2 and 5.3 below.

How likely is it you would recommen us to a friend?

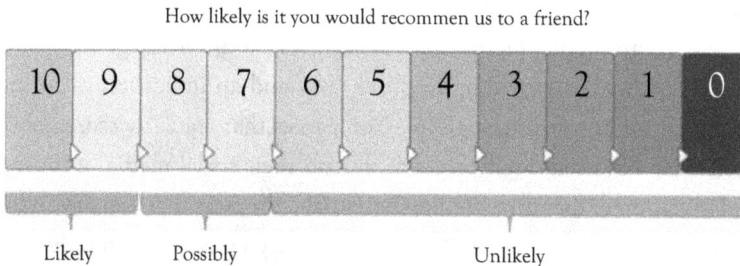

| 10 | 9 | 8 | 7 | 6 | 5 | 4 | 3 | 2 | 1 | 0 |

Likely   Possibly   Unlikely

Figure 5.2 The Net Promotor Score

The responses deliver three groups:

- Promoters: Loyal customers who may make repeat purchases and refer your brand to friends and family.
- Passives: Customers who are likely to move to a competitor if they find better price, product, or features.
- Detractors: Customers who are unsatisfied and likely to leave a negative review.

One may be given for thinking the groups are split evenly across the scoring range. However, 80 percent of negative comments will come from the bottom 60 percent (in score terms) of your customers. Therefore, we must put all those scoring 6 and below (60 and below) as Detractors. The remaining scores are split evenly between Passives and Promoters.

If you think the deck is stacked against you that would be true. However, how often do we go out of our way to complain about something or how often do we mention to friends, colleagues, and associates about a bad experience? By comparison how often do we do the same for a good experience?

Calculating NPS is a simple formula:

$$\frac{\text{Number of promoters} - \text{Number of detractors}}{\text{Total number of responses}} \times 100$$

Figure 5.3 Calculating NPS

Any NPS score >0 should be considered good. It means that you have more positively biased customers than negatively. An NPS score of >2 is "favorable." However, all scores vary by industry sector, and, as we have mentioned previously, social, and cultural effects. A score of >5 should be considered an excellent score and anything >8 exceptionally good.

NPS as well as providing feedback now and an indication of future potential can be a marketing tool. Companies that regularly score above 8 on their NPS may well promote this on their social media, websites, and in customer literature. Telling potential customers that you have a lot of customers already that really rate and value your service can only be a positive thing.

Improving a company's NPS can involve many things. The products and services for one thing need to be what the customer wants but it needs to be matched by the customer service and the relationship you have with your customers. Such is the importance of a high NPS score that there are now consultancy businesses built around just this one element of sales and marketing.

Whether you choose to use scoring or not depends on how many customers you have, how often you interact with them, and what you intend to do with the data. What kind of score is also down to your needs for the data and the relationship you have with your customer. Simply saying thank you and asking if everything is up to standard in a shop may be far more productive than asking shoppers to complete questionnaires before they leave with their bag of groceries.

Key Takeaways

It is all too easy for customers to complain about their suppliers. With the explosion of the Internet and of social media often, the first resort is not the supplier to affect improvements but to other potential customers to gain leverage in future discussions and negotiations. This may seem an unfair advantage to the customer, but it just means salespeople and the companies they represent must work harder to retain their edge.

A good CES will tell you how the sales experience went, how the sale and delivery went and the all-important first impressions of doing business. Where salespeople are concerned this is the most critical as it tells the Sales Manager about the sale itself and immediately after.

Even though CES is the first score in the series of scores we can apply. It is a specific measure unlike CSAT which is a more general measure, and perhaps also more subjective. Whether scores are determined through online questionnaires, phone calls, or face to face perhaps reflect the nature of the product or service and the type of business. It also matters whom one asks to complete such a questionnaire, and for that, we may want an independent group within the business, rather than the salesperson picking only those that will give the best scores.

Customer Satisfaction is important in understanding how customers feel today about the product or service and how that is likely to change over time. It provides an effective feedback loop for the salesperson on their own performance and that of their team and their product or service.

All companies should measure their CSAT, whether they publish and promote the findings or not. It should also be a regular and ongoing exercise to ensure constant improvements are made and the company continues to move forward. Where it is recorded, perhaps a CRM system. It can also be used as a measure to reward salespeople and Account Managements and form part of their bonus.

CHAPTER 6

CRM Is an Attitude, Not a System

Overview

When one hears the acronym CRM, one is immediately drawn to a piece of software that records who the customer is and when we last spoke to them or the copy of a recent e-mail. That is true in that a Customer Relationship Management (CRM) System does record interactions with a customer but if one thinks of CRM only as a piece of software then a significant part of what a CRM System can do for a company is lost.

The critical element of a CRM System is the data and, equally, so the recording and accuracy of that data. Capturing not just the exchanges between customer and supplier but critical data such as the contact's preferences, their position within the hierarchy of the company and their role and influence within any buying situation.

Knowing who the contact is and their complex relationship with their peers and colleagues, both individually and organizationally, as well as us as a supplier and that relationship all come to provide a rich picture of what matters to each contact and whether we are taking the right approach.

A CRM System has several key elements besides the data. The process that sits around the data ensure consistency of approach and consistency of scoring and evaluating. Reporting and dashboards provide easy insight into progress and allow critical decision making.

While CRM Systems are seen as mainly used by salespeople, they are perhaps the main contributor, closely followed by Marketing and lead generation teams. But salespeople are not the only major consumer of CRM System outputs. The data and conclusions can shape product development, which sales to pursue and even new markets or the closure of some products and markets.

Because CRM Systems offer such a wide opportunity implementing one needs to be done with the consensus not only of the users and those inputting the data but those that have most to gain from extracting the data too. Sales is a team sport, and the players need to align with the playbook. The playbook is written in a language called CRM.

CRM Is a Functional Tool

According to Microsoft cofounder and ex-Chairman Bill Gates:

The most meaningful way to differentiate your company from your competitors, the best way to put distance between you and the crowd is to do an outstanding job with information. How you gather manage and use information will determine whether you win or lose.

As we saw earlier with Rolodex and other systems, CRM has been around for some time. Today, however, a CRM System (CRM for short) is an online tool with multiple ways of interrogating the stored data. That did not happen until the 1990s when one of the first pioneers, Tom Siebel left Oracle having failed to convince them to see their own in-house system as a CRM tool. In truth, they were more sales process automation than the full-blown suite of tools we know today.

Fast forward and the business of today absolutely needs a CRM System. But that does not mean spending a large amount of the company's money on a complex or bespoke piece of software. CRM Systems can be purchased or subscribed to for little and configured to the company needs. A simple spreadsheet makes an effective, but not ideal, CRM for small companies and start-ups.

CRMs offer us the opportunity to develop foresight into the wider impact for the company in pursuing new sales opportunities. A CRM offers sales automation and is used by more than just the sales team. It allows forecasting of likely wins and therefore the potential future demand. This, in turn, helps the supply chain management. It allows tracking of conversations and can direct marketing effort. It even helps in identifying revenue possibilities and financial planning. Finally, it can even help give insight into future product development.

A CRM will provide workflow automation and the streamlining of processes which ultimately help in reducing cost. Workflow automation saves time and energy and allows wide sharing of information and avoids duplication and multiple versions of the truth.

A CRM plays an important role in providing reports on the business or data to other parts of the business for them to report. Business reporting allows a company to identify the status of a company at any given point of time. Business reporting as a component of CRM provides instant and accurate access to information, provided those inputting the data are doing this properly. It, therefore, needs to be easy to use and mobile enabled. The best CRMs allow immediate updates simply and effectively. Make it a complex tool to use and salespeople will not use and everything that follows will fail.

As a general principle, there are four ways to approach CRM. Of course, for large organizations, CRM is a strategic tool. With lots of customers, a large company needs to have a customer-centric approach to maintain effective sales performance.

For many companies, a CRM System is more of an operational tool. It allows the various functions within the business to work together, share information, and to have a consistent view of the customer. As a tool it brings together the sales process, data capture, and information sharing. It ensures the recorded view of the prospect is the current view. This facilitates marketing automation and gives marketers insight into what they can do to improve sales performance as well as measure the success of previous campaigns.

As an analytical tool alone, a CRM provides data on the number of calls, the success rate, what products and services attract the most interest, some customer type information, and what campaigns have generated the most interest. Other data points can likely be extracted but, for the most part it is more akin to a funnel measurement tool and data store than a full-suite CRM System.

CRM Systems offer a good collaboration tool built around customer data. Capturing the data from customers, from lead generation, and other sources, allows various teams within an organization to work more effectively in their own function. Sharing common data and updating the database accordingly in a way that is less about funnel management and certainly less than an operational tool or a strategic system.

For something more than the basic elements of data capture and collaboration a CRM, no matter how good, requires several other elements to be successful:

- The rules built into the system
- Process and process-governance
- Reporting and analytics
- Quality and accuracy of data
- Commitment to use it
- Access anywhere

Before we get too far into this, if you have no system in place, or the one you have is no longer up to the task, there is a decision on whether to have a CRM System or an Opportunity Tracking System (OTS).

An OTS according to Kapture:

… lets you coordinate and consolidate your entire sales responsibilities through a single unified process. By integrating different sales processes, you can channelize the link of activities that ensure timely execution of each process.

Kapture argues a CRM System will:

… augment and improve your existing business operations to achieve higher operational efficiency and scalability. Ideally, a CRM software should comprehensively connect the different business touch points to streamline the flow of operations and data to achieve the best results.

Based on these two descriptions, it would seem most people have a CRM operating as an OTS and very few people have bought an OTS! And if that is not confusing enough, the choice now for systems and the wide variety of their capabilities make choosing the right one a complex task. In fact, for some industries for example, event management, health care, or government to name but three; there are specialist CRM Systems just for the task—these tend to be closer to *Kapture*'s definition of what is a true CRM.

Putting aside OTS versus CRM and individual needs or industry-specific requirements, the idea of a system to track and measure progress, record data, share information, provide insight, and offer informed decision making; are all key requirements of a good CRM/OTS.

What Should a CRM Look Like?

A CRM is a functional tool that holds information on the client contact, the client company, the sales opportunity, and anything that relates to or supports the sales pursuit. Extracting from it are reports too.

Some organizations even have product configurators built into their CRM, contract and document management, postsale project management, and cross-team collaboration tools. In 2020 *Salesforce*, the world's largest CRM System provider, bought *Slack*, a collaborating and messaging application, for $27.7 billion. The size of the deal demonstrates how big the CRM industry now is, a long way from the *Rolodex* of 1956.

More importantly, *Salesforce* bought *Slack* because they recognized the growing need for greater collaboration within business. Salespeople need to be kept up to date, get help and support, share information, and be kept informed simply and efficiently, at the desk or on the road. Any CRM System needs to deliver sales performance not just data tracking and it needs to be done with minimal burden to all the users.

The core elements of any CRM are the contact, the organization, and the sale. For most companies with 100 to 500 employees, up to seven people are likely to be involved in the buying decision. Some are influencers, others are user-representatives, some financial evaluators, and others business evaluators.

Having a methodology that allows you to identify and work all of those involved in a buying decision requires a methodological approach and a tool to help keep all these plates spinning until you win the deal is perhaps a good thing to have.

A good CRM will allow information on buyers and contacts to be entered into the system. More than just the basic contact information but background information on their interests and an organizational structure, even if not graphically displayed. For complex organizations, this structure extends beyond the team and company personnel structure but possibly even the company's structure.

Keeping this up to date with details of meetings and conversations is vital when it comes to the sales pursuit. Structuring then the system that allows an update for an individual to be assigned also to a company and to an opportunity ensures all the data can be surfaced to the user as needed regardless of whether the user is looking at the customer contact or the sales opportunity.

A sales opportunity begins with qualification. Knowing something about the account and who the contacts are to continue a dialogue and the fact they may have need or use of your product or services.

When a dialogue has been opened, you are more likely to find out about an opportunity sooner, rather than be invited to tender later in the process perhaps. Having access to contacts and forecasting the process of a likely opportunity later allows you to influence the process.

The opportunity itself will be tracked and managed in the CRM. Following a set of steps to make sure, it stays qualified or passes through decision gates is part of the structure of a CRM System. Often, built into the CRM, will be qualifying questionnaires and steps that need to be completed to proceed to the next stage.

CRM Systems give visibility to your sales pipeline by providing real-time overview of where all the opportunities sit through the process, allowing informed decisions to be made.

A good Opportunity Management system—technology, tools, process, and data—will improve your likelihood of winning more business, allow you to focus effort and resources when needed and where needed, and provide high-level planning data for other parts of the business.

If the first you see of a sales opportunity is when you receive the bid document, you are already too late. Do not get excited that you have been invited to the party, it was a last-minute invite and that is either because someone dropped out or because they need someone to fill the empty spaces.

The Importance of Data

It goes without saying a CRM without data is about as effective as telescopic sights on a knife. Capturing data as well as maintaining data is key, but it must be done within the confines of every stricter data privacy rules.

In April 2016, the European Union rolled out the General Data Protection Regulation (GDPR). It came into being two years later and changed to an enormous degree what data companies can store, how they are allowed to process it, and the length of time they can keep it. To go into GDPR in detail would take a lot of time, but there are a few basic principles that it pays to understand.

Why does a European Union Regulation matter to more than just the EU? While it may be an EU Regulation, it applies to more than just EU companies and more than just EU citizens. Any company operating in or supplying to customers of the European Union (and other countries that have adopted the standards) need to be aware of GDPR.

Following GDPR, many countries adopted similar regulations or updated and amended their current data privacy and protection rules to follow more closely what the EU set out. The EU, having set the bar high has started a process to better protect the individual.

In 2019, *Google LLC* (an American company) was fined €50 million by the French Commission for "Informatics and Liberty" because of a GDPR breach. *Marriott Hotels* has been fined twice for breaches of GDPR regulations. Plus, many more and more than a few more than once. While most fines have been for European companies or individuals (including a police officer and a sitting Mayor), the regulations are meant not just for EU companies.

Maintaining information on an individual needs to be relevant to the needs of the company and/or individual using the data. For example, a general retailer knowing your religious beliefs is hardly relevant. A hospital knowing your sexual preferences though perhaps useful in certain circumstances is generally considered irrelevant. Likewise, your life insurance company may well have good cause to know your medical history, alcohol, tobacco, and substance abuse it does not mean they should pass that on to your property insurance or motor vehicle insurance company.

CRM Systems, therefore, need to be good at capturing the data needed in the pursuit of a good sales opportunity but not overstep the mark.

All this is well and good provided the customer lets you keep the data in the first place. The GDPR principle of Erasure (the right to be forgotten). But even before we get there the customer/contact must expressly give you permission to keep and use his or her data.

Simply handing over a business card does not give you the right to store all this information. Of course, it would be a bit churlish of a potential new customer to ask you to not keep any information on them while still wanting to do business with you. But for prospects and people, you want to pursue that are not yet customers you need to get their express permission to keep their data.

Purchasing data is often only the start, what happens next is the responsibility of everyone involved in the sales pursuit. Marketing may update records based on events and reactions, responses to campaigns and from research completed and knowledge gained. For the most part, however, it is the salesperson who will be charged with keeping the CRM up to date.

Rules, Process, Governance

To ensure consistency, common guidelines or a rulebook is needed. Everyone will know how to input names and addresses of course; but how you score the success of a follow up, the way you value an opportunity, the stages the opportunity has reached, how you score the customer loyalty. What constitutes a good contact versus bad? Between all these are nuances and gradings. It does not have to be a perfect science to get right every time but there does need to be a common understanding that everyone buys into.

Good CRMs have structured workflows that can be tailored, at least to some degree, to suit the needs of the user community. What the salespeople want and how they interact with it will be different to what forecasters are using it for or what the lead generation and marketing teams are putting into, or taking out of, the system.

For most CRMs today, there is a limited amount of workflow configuration available but for more complex, and likely more expensive, systems then a significant amount of configuration can be achieved.

The large number of general CRMs available today would suit most businesses but, for some industries, specialist CRM Systems are needed. I have worked on CRM projects in the major customer events industry and insurance broking industry, both requiring CRM Systems specifically built for those industries.

For small enterprises, CRMs are typically little more than contact database and diary management with perhaps a small element of product interest content. In such cases, numerous products exist such is the success today of those early CRM development companies such as *Siebel, Salesforce,* and *ACT!*

For larger organizations, governance is important in any successful implementation and use of a CRM System. Unlike expenses where, if you do not fill in your form you do not get paid, failing to keep up to date a CRM will not be noticed straight away and will have a far wider impact that just one person's income.

Making sure CRM Systems are kept up to date and done so consistently and accurately falls to all the users. For large organizations, however, this can be a significant task just to make sure everyone is doing their job.

Managing the accuracy and availability, as well as security and consistency, of any CRM System, like any other complex database, is Data Governance. The parts that make up Data Governance of course include the quality of the data and where best to source it, both ethically and for relevance (accuracy and usefulness). It also includes data security and user access. The policies the users of the system and the company generally use the data needs to be clearly understood. The type and availability of reports, not everyone should have access to all data points and all reports, also forms part of the CRM System governance.

Data Governance needs to be considered at the start of any project, see Figure 6.1. It formulates how to structure the data, the teams, and the processes as well as how to source and manage data and how best to extract the most from a core system.

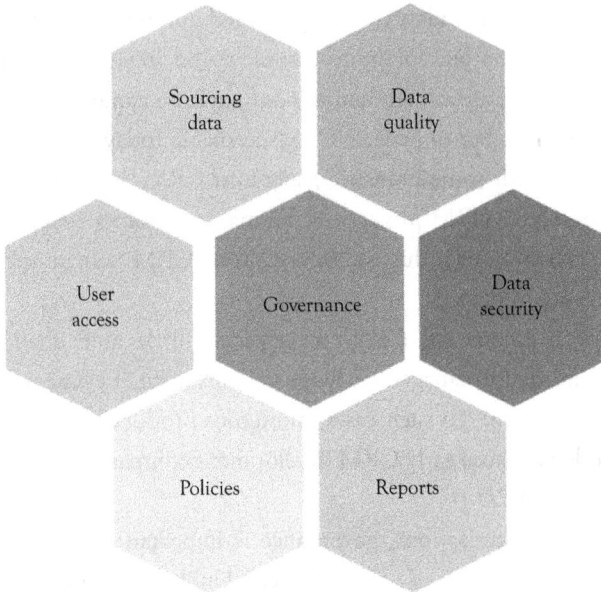

Figure 6.1 **CRM Data Governance**

Data in a CRM System can be broken down into baseline data and actionable data. Baseline would include company and personal details, and general opportunity detail. Actionable data is the data that helps move the sales pursuit forward and requires adding to and updating as we learn more about the opportunity.

Cataloguing the data correctly at the start with a simple and effective structure for recording information will make it easier for all users to keep up to date and prevent multiple copies of the same information. It will still happen that you end up with two of something but to try and minimize it with a simple and effective organizational/company structure for the database will make a big difference to how much data cleanse is needed later.

The definitions of all the key parameters are important as are the policies that you wish people to use when entering and updating data. Being consistent across multiple users from different departments will significantly help improve the effectiveness of a CRM System.

More than anything, Governance requires the commitment of all to ensure the system is accurate and clean of all manner of errors and omissions. Having representatives in each department responsible for this will help and making it everyone's responsibility is important. Despite all this, there will still likely need to be regular data sweeps and clean ups.

The Rules and Processes a company has on how to update a CRM System will help ensure the amount of duplication, rework, data cleansing, and someone else inputting data that the right person was too lazy, is reduced to a minimum. Sharing responsibility to all and making everyone equally accountable will help.

CRM Systems fail because a handful of people have decided not to use it or do the bare minimum because they must and do not see the value in the tool. However, the biggest CRM System failures are because the user interface is not as good as it should be, and the way data is entered, and the structure imposed on the users made it an unfriendly tool.

Rules, Process, and Governance are all vital tools in the success of a CRM System, but a lot of that can be addressed in the way the solution is deployed, managed, and how easy it is to use. The more effective the system is in the design stage and getting users to complete the information, the less is needed to manage the system when it is up and running across the business.

Reporting and Analytics

Before we begin, let us be clear. Reporting, Management Information, and Analytics are not limited to a CRM System. In addition to data from a CRM System, there will be financial information and nonsales or product Key Performance Indicators. However, in the context of sales, sales performance, and sales management, the CRM System should be the richest source of data. For that reason alone, Reporting and Analytics is an extension of the CRM System supplemented by other sources of data.

To best explain the difference between Reporting and Analytics, this description from *Visier Inc.* which sums it up perfectly: *"Reports provide data; analytics provide insight."*

A report will, typically, organize information (data), provide a summary and allow some assessment. It can give indication of performance and provide comparisons.

Extracting meaningful insights from the data to help understand more fully is the process of analytics. Where reporting may give the what, analytics provides the why and, more importantly, provides direction on where next.

Most CRM Systems have the capability to present different types of "Dashboards." That is the critical pieces of data to that function presented in a simple single page format. A useful presentation of what matters to a Sales Manager is different to that needed by the salesperson or marketing teams and so on.

Simple CRM Systems may lack the sophistication of analytical reporting, so often there exists export capabilities to other online tools sometimes pushed automatically, for others you must extract the data and produce a report.

The best CRM reporting tools tend to show data on the value of the pipeline at each stage, either in total value or weighted by win likelihood (assessed by the salesperson), the length of time opportunities have been opened and average sales cycle time, the total value of the pipeline, weighted by the stage at which each opportunity is, new versus renewal opportunities, calendar, overdue tasks, cost of sale to date. For Sales Managers, performance against target of each team member, time spent on each opportunity, stage of opportunity by team member, cost/expense by opportunity, forecast by team member, team and overall, ratios of progress from stage to stage by each team member, product mix of sales opportunities.

CRM Reporting and Analytics provides insight and allows better decision making. Focusing on what works best and what is draining time and effort to achieve a better result, identifying where there are consistent obstacles or opportunities, both within the product sale and the salesperson leads to better performance.

Reporting from a CRM System should be a simple extraction to provide immediate insight. In some larger organizations, fully one day a week of a Sales Manager's time is spent producing reports, analyzing performance, and chasing for updates. Sales Manager are supporting the sale and helping salespeople win more business.

Implementing CRM

Implementing a CRM solution is not just another internal IT project. Indeed, almost the opposite, see Figure 6.2. It is very much people first and process and certainly not an IT project.

Critical in the success is not to change the way people work. Processes may need to change, some additional discipline and structure required but it needs to work alongside and with what people do as part of their daily routine and not impose a whole new way of working.

However, a CRM System will challenge some operational models and some approaches to how people work and think, and the nature of their day. Therefore, it is vital any project is not imposed from the top but delivered across the business with buy-in at every level and in every department.

Simply implementing a system and dictating a process will not guarantee business success and sales growth. Even with all the other elements in place a CRM will only work if the entire sales team and those more widely using it, whether to input or extract data, are committed to the project, and see the value in it.

A report by *Superoffice* showed that 30 to 65 percent of CRM projects fail and less than 40 percent of CRM projects demonstrate full scale end-user adoption. The main reasons for such poor adoption rates have little to do with technology.

A CRM is perhaps seen as a sales tool, but it involves all parts of an organization. When determining which CRM, those departments with the most to offer and most to gain should be involved and management as well as users engaged in the decision process on which CRM to use.

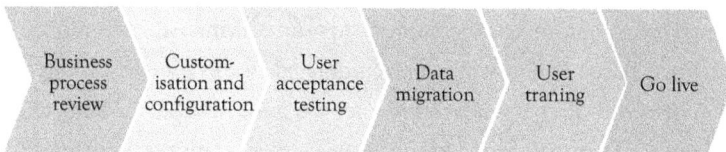

Figure 6.2 Implementing CRM

The right CRM project implementation team includes not just those selecting the tool but those implementing it. For large organizations, this may fall to a small team usually led by a project manager. For smaller organizations, one individual perhaps more. The implementation team needs to balance the needs of all the individuals versus what is achievable and manage the conflicting demands that will likely arise.

I was working at a very well regarded large international organization that had, a year earlier, implemented a new CRM. The system was selected exclusively by the Finance Department and plugged into their entire supply chain and finance system. Every person involved in sales had their commission directly calculated from the system and every order had to be placed in the system.

The nature of the products and services for sale were, in part, regulated and each order was configured for the customer needs. All in all, it was a complex supply chain and ordering system. For these reasons, the Finance Department took charge of selecting and then designing and implementing the system.

At no point through the design and development process were the sales-team involved. Sales Managers were simply told a new system was coming. From the sales user it was a simply dreadful tool to use. Salespeople could not see the data presented in the easy way that helped your job, they could not produce reports that helped them organize their day or week and the Sales Managers had insight into financial performance and supply chain only.

The entire process became so bad that if any salesperson failed several daily routine tasks or if one follow-up was missed, one update not done, or one task step not completed in the allotted number of days the salesperson received a report, as did the Sales Manager. Lots of red ink in the electronic report and even monthly scores of the worst 'offenders' and the worst offending teams and regions.

Failure to follow this rigid protocol also impacted people's commission if some steps were missed your customer order was not completed. Because the system was built around finance and not the sales process or customer satisfaction. If there was an issue with the supply chain due to incomplete details on the order or incorrect information the salesperson was not informed.

The net result was the order handling team because the go-to department for order updates. They spent more time handling calls from salespeople than they did keeping the supply of goods and services moving. The salespeople hated the system and used it as sparingly as possible and provided as little input as possible. What should have been a leap forward in customer relationships, sales management and improved insight became a stick by which the Finance Department would beat every other department.

A year after it had been implemented, I met the Group FD for this and went through all the reasons why and what could be done without having to completely reinvent the system or implement some better technology. The outcome was to be expected. A Finance Director that chose the system without considering the needs of the company and the users cared little for all my observations, despite the fact he was paying for my time.

Not only was the original decision flawed in its process and those involved. The company chose to ignore the errors and pursue what was a failing system because those that made the decision were unwilling to accept it was failing. Failure is only an opportunity to learn if you listen to the failure and put in corrective action.

The success of your CRM is not just down to selecting the right provider, working through the process and internal data structure, and then implementing. It matters after that, that users have someone to contact for help. Less so a helpdesk more a superuser.

For large organizations, a helpdesk may be required but often it is one of the members of the wider team. Less so one of the frontline salespeople, perhaps someone from sales admin/support, or within the marketing team.

Having a power user, a knowledgeable advocate if you will, a person users can go to with questions, refresh informal training, and to make suggestions is an important part of the continued success of any CRM implementation.

CRM is also not just a system and process it is a new way of doing things. Built around the structure and process, there needs to be methodologies and, potentially, other tools and systems. We have talked already about some of these additional processes tools and will continue to do so. But it is a two-way street. Additional tools and systems, processes and the way people work must dovetail with your CRM System and, more importantly, your CRM has to fit into what people do, the processes they are familiar with, and other systems they use today.

Effective training on how to use the CRM will ensure users and receivers of information from the system understand the wider use and the importance of the system. They will get to appreciate why and how things are scored and how it fits into their role. Potentially also why some long-standing practices have had to change.

Training is more than an online webinar or watch and learn video or more than half a day in the classroom. It does need to have some "sheep dip" element at first but there needs to be available to hand tools and tips, potentially as we have discussed earlier a User Champion and access to refresher training.

A CRM implementation project must draw out negative attitudes and opinions. The team leading the implementation needs to have these out in the open and deal with them. To counter these, the company needs not only cast-iron arguments on why the business needs this and why the user should do it, but softer reasons that appeal to users' specific interests. Taking an objection and countering with a business-centre-led argument is not enough. Dealing with objections and obstacles and finding a positive solution that will sate the user is critical to long-term success.

Some companies make CRM updates part of the individuals' key objectives. Simplifying some tasks for a user is key in winning over those not in favor. Integration with e-mail and diary can help, generating new leads through the system so it becomes part of a daily ritual can all help.

A client of mine had previously implemented a CRM system. Some of the salespeople thought it a good idea and others had a "we have not needed one before" philosophy. However, the company was growing and perhaps there was some argument to having a system bearing in mind the increasing size and scale of the company and the complexity of their products.

It was agreed by all, however, that some structure was needed and a common approach to how they record data and how they segment customers and products. The salespeople and wider members of the process agreed to use a structured approach and shared spreadsheets to keep record and share information. What the objectors had failed to realize was a spreadsheet used in this way is a CRM.

Once adopted, over time, the spreadsheet became a little more involved. As the company grew people were using it more and more and began to develop their own add-ins to the sheet.

When the time was right, we began looking at a new CRM system. From the very start we engaged with the team and got them to see the benefits of migrating what they were doing on a spreadsheet to something that was the same in structure but easier to share and keep updated and that integrated with other systems so less duplicating of data. Even at this stage there were still objectors but the process of getting everyone on board was complete and a new system was implemented successfully.

A CRM implementation is like any other project in many regards. However, its success or failure depends on a wide range of people in multiple departments all with different approaches and attitudes. For this reason, companies need not only treat it as a project but also as a sale.

Selling the reasons, the benefits and putting together an internal marketing plan to sell the benefits of a new CRM System and processes are often key to the success of such a project. This may seem overkill, but it does not cost much money and is not a heavy burden on time. However, if the project fails what is the cost and time wasted by comparison?

Every CRM System failure I have seen was down to not taking the team with you through the design and implementation, and even the selection process. Salespeople will be the main users, so it makes sense to engage them early on. Treat a new CRM project as if it were a sale and follow the sales methodology!

Once implemented, treat the users as you would customers and keep them onside. Take on board suggestions, but do not promise to satisfy every whim and idea and make sure you conduct regular feedback. Above all, however, with a CRM System it really is *rubbish in = rubbish out* and the people mostly putting data in are the salespeople, so if it does not work ultimately, it will be the salespeople that are to blame, but do not be surprised if they blame the system!

Key Takeaways

Going into any game without the team having a plan and knowing that the game plan of the opposition may work at an amateur level in sport but, in the professional world of sport, it matters that we play as one team and the sum of the parts make up more than the whole. For those playing their sport at the highest level and winning nothing is left to chance. Every weakness and strength identified both for our team and for the opposition.

The CRM System contains every previous win or defeat, it contains every player profile, and it rates us on how we stack up against the opposition. It tells us how to play the game and it lets us tune our game plan to win. As the clock ticks down through the game, our CRM System tells us where we need to change tactics and whether we need to make substitutes.

Analyzed and scrutinized by the coaches and those on the side-lines, it feeds back to the players on the pitch, admittedly not always well received.

CRM at its heart may be a piece of software but it is the broader understanding of the term that separates companies using it to keep track of sales pursuits and those tuning it to achieve sales excellence.

Process and governance in any CRM System are critical but most critical of all is the data within. Rubbish in = Rubbish out may be a well-known phrase and for a CRM System this is absolutely true.

What data is needed and how it is tracked is often dictated to by the company itself and by the needs of each sales pursuit. Some complex sales require much more data capture on a broader range of topics for more people than sales pursuits of an altogether simpler nature. What processes are chosen to manage the CRM System are likewise a construct of the customer, the product or service, and the complexity of the sale.

The single critical element that will determine the success or not of a CRM are the people that use it, whether to input data or to extract meaning. Selection of a system, data elements required and the process that pulls this together needs be through a cross-functional team that ensures it attracts the right attitude from the users. If a CRM System is implemented and fails to attract the right response, it will have failed and almost always impossible to fix except by force.

A good CRM empowers the salespeople and provides insight to the business. It educates Marketing and it informs Sales. It allows sharper decision making through improved efficiency with greater consistency. That a CRM can do all that indicates just how significant this is and why getting it right across all elements is vital to the overall success of the sales pursuits.

CHAPTER 7

Channel Sales

Overview

Historically, Channel Sales was seen as the way third parties would sell on behalf of another company. The company may implement a channel sales strategy to sell products and services via dealers, retailers, and affiliates. Today, however, this is ever more common through Online Sales. Multichannel sales involve selling through a variety of different methods. Omnichannel, another phrase often used, is much the same as multiple channel sales but where the different methods combine and lead to a seamless experience regardless of how the customer interacts and at what stage.

Omnichannel allows the customer to engage online whether to research, browse or buy, and to do the same through third-party platforms or directly in a shop. The customer can pick and choose which parts of the buying process are conducted in person in store and which are conducted virtually and online, mobile or computer. A customer may research online first, visit the shop to evaluate in person and then order online for later delivery. All should be seamless and, aside from the obvious differences, it should not matter how the customer engages to ensure consistency. Done well this leads to more sales, better customer satisfaction, and greater customer loyalty.

Whether as a preferred model, or as an additional model, whether applied generically, or only in some markets or territories the Sales Channel approach allows greater flexibility and, in many cases, a lower risk option for entering or developing new markets. Many businesses today operate exclusively through an alternative channel strategy.

Whether it is a franchising model or relying on sales agents, retailers, and partners, it is not uncommon to find companies that operate exclusively through the Indirect Channel only. Franchising in fast food retail is particularly common with over 90 percent of *Subway* and 82 percent of *McDonalds* being franchises worldwide today. However, there is more to the Indirect Channel than franchising alone.

Types of Indirect Sales Channel

Retailing is the most obvious and common Indirect Sales Channel. Manufacturers produce goods and eventually it is sold to consumers through such a channel.

In the world of B2B and corporate selling, the Indirect Channel Sales Model differs little from the retailer model save perhaps for the relationship balance between producer and seller and the types of models available. In the supermarket retailer model and the online partner retailer model, the channel is very often all powerful whereas in the higher-end corporate sales model this is less the case.

Indirect Channel Sales can be complex to manage. Managing the different types of Channel Partners and what they add to the sale while ensuring the product or service remains relatively consistent to the end customer may require a whole team of itself to manage.

There are many variants to Channel Partnerships and some work better than others depending on the nature of your business and the market. Below is a list of the channels companies can choose:

- Traditional Resellers
- Affiliate Partners and Distributors
- Wholesalers
- Value-Added Reseller (VAR)
- Traditional Retailers
- Agents
- Franchise
- Consultants
- Reverse Channel
- Online Channels

Today, most companies have some form of Indirect Channel Sales and, for the most part, a simple, **Traditional Reseller**. A company or individual not employed by the manufacturer to act as a sales agent. The role may be purely a commission role and, for individuals, they would be self-employed. For a company acting as a traditional reseller, it gives the parent organization the opportunity to enter new markets at low cost or cover more ground more effectively rather than employ an army of salespeople.

Very often resellers are required to purchase the product first before reselling, perhaps less so where software is sold, usually via outbound marketing and telesales. Traditional (not retail) resellers are purely about the sale, the delivery, distribution, and other parts of the process, as well as customer service and satisfaction fall to the company providing the solution itself.

Distributors and **Affiliates** provide a reseller partnership where the manufacturer will pay commission to businesses, and individuals who promote and sell their products. Affiliate Partners are typically paid a percentage of each sale they deliver. It is a very simple model that allows the manufacturer to develop a large sales team quickly with low cost. However, control of the message and the quality and professionalism of the agent is not something easily controlled.

Affiliate Partnerships tend to work best for simple products that require little quality checks and very little after-sales and customer care. Focused more on "box shifting" than solution selling.

Small companies and large can have such programs and very often done through remote selling or online. For example, *Amazon* has an Affiliate Program where their products are promoted on or through other websites. If the third-party website sells the product then the Affiliate is rewarded on a commission basis.

The traditional supply chain is made up of a manufacturer selling to a wholesaler, selling to a retailer, and selling to the customer. For most industries that still applies today although in many industries also large players have vertically integrated and moved from retailing alone to buying direct from the manufacturer and taking ownership all the way through to the end sale. This is particularly true of grocery retailing where the larger players now have buyers or buying agents around the globe buying from the farmers and cooperatives the raw ingredients of the everyday shopping basket.

We rarely think of a **Wholesaler** as an Indirect Channel Sale. It allows the supplier to split between different pricing strategies for bulk sales and traditional direct sales. Wholesalers have the capacity to distribute in volume, of course, and that can offer significant appeal. While it does not require any form of relationship with the end retailer, it does remove you farther from your customer and, where customer service is concerned that may make it more difficult to manage the end customer relationship.

VARs are more likely to be technology companies. Often purchasing software and then adding additional features or function repackaging and then selling to the end customer. Or perhaps a company that is a hardware reseller that takes on software as well and sells as a complete solution including service, support, and maintenance.

Traditional Retail is still the most popular form of Channel Sale. We may not think of Retail as a separate Sales Channel because, for the most part, it is how the business-to-consumer (B2C) world of sales operates.

Within the Retail Channel, there are options to develop alternative market offerings. The same product can be sold in one shop for a set price: repackaged and repriced and sold in a different shop. Traditional retail offers control over the supply/distribution chain and limits the supply of goods at certain times or in certain markets.

A Sales Agent does not take ownership of the product or service before selling on but acts on behalf of the supplier to sell the product and create a purchase agreement between the supplier/manufacturer and the end customer. They are, in effect, an introducer and negotiator to the sale and work to complete the sales agreement between the customer and the supplier.

In the UK, one of the largest providers of Merchant Services (the card payment systems you see in shops) employs almost exclusively Sales Agents to sell its products and services to retailers.

Franchising has evolved today from 17th century ferry operators and even before that perhaps. Today, however, it is a very well-structured process with a franchisor and franchisees and operates around the globe. It allows a company to scale quickly but for a slice of the profits and brings together both parties in a way that differs to the traditional supplier–retailer.

The Franchisee must abide by the rules of the franchisor and must pay to join the association. The branding, promotion, distribution, and often the internal business systems are controlled from the center and, in that way, binds both parties to a common purpose.

Aside from a Master Franchisor, where a franchisee recruits their own franchises in a specific territory, there are two different types of franchising. The most common is Business Format Franchising. The franchisor provides to the franchisee its trade name, products, and services, as well as help with business start-up, training, branding, quality control, marketing, and business advice.

Product Distribution Franchising is less common in the numbers of franchise owners but is often larger in total sales. We think of this in the main as manufacturing industries, for example a soft drinks manufacturer may have a bottling franchise or a drugs developer a manufacturing franchise.

Consultants are included, although one could argue they are not part of the Indirect Sales Channel. However, whether they are tied consultants, meaning they have a relationship with their product supplier to promote and support your product or service; or if they are independent consultants, they still help the customer make the buying decision. They may get involved in some of the commercial discussions. Accepted they will go into negotiations representing the client more than the supplier, but they will want to see a positive outcome and so have a vested interest in making sure the negotiation is a success. They may need to be treated differently to other parts of the Channel and so, to not include them, would be to neglect them.

Reverse Channel sales is not a new phenomenon but is also not that common. However, we do see more of it today. Traditional sales follow the simple manufacturer–supplier–buyer process, or variations thereof. The Reverse Channel is where a supplier purchases a product and then finds new ways to sell it using new ideas.

There are great examples of how products developed for one purpose eventually became successful in other ways. Playdough was originally a cleaning product, Listerine was originally a floor cleaner, bubble wrap was originally a wall covering. Distilling wine was a way to make transportation easier before reapplying water to turn it back into wine. Today we call it Brandy.

In the late 1960s, Spencer Silver of *The 3M Company* was trying to develop a very strong glue for the aerospace industry. A glue that sets hard becomes brittle so, one that does not set, should remain stronger. Sadly, it did not work, and he spent five years trying to find a use for a glue that can be reused and does not leave any residue when used and reused.

It took another five years for a *3M* colleague to use the glue when holding some papers together and then a few more years of development before the Post-it Note first went on sale in 1980. Accepted this is not a Reverse Channel as the idea never left the building but it does show how one idea can be taken from its original design to become something totally different.

Upcycling is a very good example of Reverse Channel Sales. Product recalls can also open a Reverse Channel, where the product cannot be used for its original purpose and now must be reused in another way to at least recoup some of the investment.

The Online Sales Channel

Online Sales Channels can be either direct or through a third-party provider. In many respects, it crosses over or mixes with other channels. One could view online as merely another form of retail. Or perhaps it could be a platform for Reverse Channel, some Franchises and Agents may be online, as too would be Affiliates, Resellers, and Distributors.

Online Sales, whether through a third party or direct, has existed since the early 1990s. In 1994, a company called *Cadabra* was incorporated, today we know it as *Amazon*. *AuctionWeb* was founded in 1995, today we call it *eBay*. However, despite the United States being leaders in the field, it did not take long for other countries to step into the market and, more recently, relatively new entrants have established themselves and grown very quickly. *Alibaba* was founded in 1999, *Flipkart* only in 2007.

There are two versions of Online Sales Channel, through a third party or directly to the consumer. Selling not through a third party is simply online retail and though it is a channel to market, it is not a separate third-party channel as the others in this chapter. Sometimes referred to as retailing or ecommerce.

Some third-party resellers hold no inventory, manufacture no products, and take no responsibility for delivery and returns. These companies provide a platform for others to use and take a small charge for their services. Companies such as *Uber*, *Trivago*, *AirBnB*, and price comparison websites offer a platform for others to promote and sell in this way.

Four variants of ecommerce are recognized today, and development of these channels is optimized to better serve mobile user or online computer-based users. The needs of the phone user and that of the computer user may be the same but the processes, structure, layout and design, and process flow, as well as operating systems require different approaches. These four types of ecommerce one can best describe as:

- Business-to-business (B2B)
- Business-to-consumer (B2C)
- Consumer-to-consumer (C2C)
- Consumer-to-business (C2B)

There is a further argument that B2A and A2B should be treated as additional channels. These are concerned with Business and Administrations, such as Government departments or local and regional authorities. Perhaps one may consider C2A and A2C. However, though these serve specific needs they should be viewed perhaps as subsets of the above four main types of ecommerce.

The most prevalent mobile form of ecommerce is banking. Today we call that Fintech, and we think of this as a new field, populated by relatively new companies, some with huge valuations. By January 2021, there were 134 Fintech Unicorns globally (a Unicorn is defined as a privately held company valued at over $1 billion). Six of these 134 were founded pre-2000—Cayan, Finicity, GreenDot, Numbrs, PayPal, and PineLabs—the remainder are all 21st Century companies.

We see Fintech as a relatively new phenomenon, but financial technology has been around since 1860 when Giovanni Caselli developed the *Pentelegraph*, used to verify signatures for banks. Swiping a credit card, using an ATM, interbank transfers, these are all fintech, but it is when the technology began to change the customer experience in this century that the term FinTech finally entered common use.

Whether mobile enabled or computer enabled the four forms of ecommerce all fulfill the same function, of allowing trade between two entities (individuals or companies). Each type of transaction requires a mix of the same elements and specific requirements to excite and entice the consumer to buy. Understanding what will engage a potential buyer is less a traditional sales function and more a marketing opportunity driven by technology to develop a sale.

Selling through the Online Channel can offer significant advantages in terms of speed to market, and low supply chain cost—"clicks not bricks." Starting in 2020, the global pandemic accelerated the need for companies to be more focused online. As retailers were forced to remain closed and those that did remain open saw less customers visiting, reaching customers in new ways, or reaching more customers through established Online Channels became paramount.

In the UK, online retail grew fivefold in 2020. Considering the UK was the leader in online shopping previously, this is a significant change. Online retail in India doubled in 2020, in the United States more than threefold, Japan almost doubled, and China 1.6 times. The importance of ecommerce is no longer just an option for any channel sales strategy.

Online Sales Channels may offer an easier way to enter new markets, to experiment with new products or services, or to adapt their market strategy to suit different markets. Previously, we have explored much of this and considered the product, in the main, to be physical. However, for service-related industries, it may be possible to be far more dynamic using Online Sales and marketing.

Whether applying the Ansoff Matrix, BCG or GE-McKinsey Matrices, or the CAGE Distance Framework to new or existing markets and new or existing products. For products that can be sold online, or potentially even delivered online, the opportunities and how to evaluate and deliver a solution change dramatically.

The challenges for the salesperson in online selling is the lack of direct customer contact. For complex sales, it applies less and, therefore, when it matters to have a good sales strategy and a good pursuit plan, it becomes less critical. However, even for the complex sale, online matters in terms of content marketing but less so on the final purchase.

For online selling, the ability to cross-sell or upsell also changes. In face-to-face meetings across a Boardroom table or at the counter of a local café, it is simple to ask a question and to have a variety of options. Online retailing requires technology to understand buyer behavior and to program options that allow alternatives and additions to be presented. Where customers are repeat customers, such as online grocery shopping, previous purchase history, and associated product buys become easier over time. For the one-off visitor, it becomes more difficult to understand what else they might buy.

Perhaps the most significant consideration for the complex sale is to think online-first. That is the first interaction the customer is likely to have will be online, whether that is researching your products and services, or those of your competitors, or researching your company, or even the personal profile of the salespeople. The Online Sales Channel may be seen as a sales channel, but it is also very often the first element of any sale.

The Sales Funnel (Chapter 1) is simplified for online retail, see Figure 7.1. Awareness and Interest combine to become Discovery. Accepted Discovery still requires Marketing to create Awareness and for the customer to show Interest, but this can be done without the need for promotion and product or brand positioning, simply by being in the market and by being competitive. Being better than the competition will get better reviewer reports.

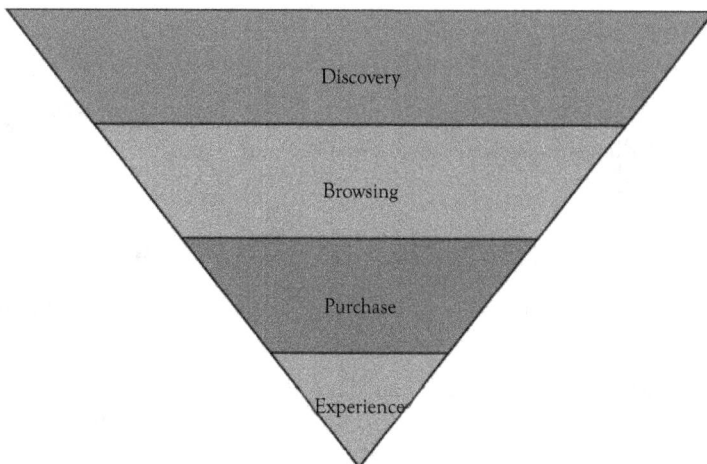

Figure 7.1 The Online Sales Funnel

Consideration and Evaluation are now done through browsing. Browsing one online offering and comparing to another, looking at reviews and reports, and looking at customer feedback and Customer Satisfaction. The decision to purchase remains. However, customer loyalty is now as much about ease of transacting online, the feeling of safety toward one's personal details and the overall experience not just the product itself.

The Online Sales Funnel is a simpler model with many elements of the traditional Sales Funnel contained therein but with sufficient differences that it requires an approach led almost exclusively by marketing and less by salespeople.

According to *Shopify*, *"Ecommerce marketing is the practice of using promotional tactics to drive traffic to your online store, converting that traffic into paying customers, and retaining those customers post-purchase."*

Shopify operates in over 150 countries providing retail direct online outlets to more than 1.7 million customers. Their view is that ecommerce and the Online Sales Channel is a marketing function rather than a sales function. This is indeed true and, as part of the channel mix it requires managing. For in-house management may be by Marketing, but for outsourced online channels and ecommerce sites, the e-channel should still be managed as a Sales Channel.

The in-house Online Sales Channel is managed most often by a division of Marketing and requires a focus on product availability, returns management, and the supply chain. As such, it is not a sales channel that requires sales management.

External ecommerce should perhaps be treated the same as for other sales channels but with less direct involvement from the Sales Manager and more direct engagement with the marketing team.

Managing the Indirect Sales Channel

Sales Channels, other than ecommerce, may not be the first choice but for many companies. However, it represents an efficient way to expand, enter new territories, or to balance the risk of investing in direct sales versus a lack of control from indirect sales.

Indirect Channel Sales will reduce profits on sales, but perhaps not total profits. Sales forecasting, and control over your reputation is important, so it matters to have in place the right model and manage it well. Empower the Indirect Sales Channel to success and control the impact they can have to the overall business, its values, brand, and customer relationships.

The first thing needed in Indirect Channel Sales is a clearly defined and understood product or service. Accepting the Indirect Channel Sales may want to put their own spin on things and sell it their way but the tighter the control over what the product or service is the less chance of failure, misrepresentation, and impact on your brand, your company, and the product.

A Channel Sales Manager is often key to the success of Indirect Channel Sales. They own the relationship between the manufacturer and the Channel Partners, they ensure the Channel has everything they need to be successful and monitor for failing performance and reward for good. The Channel Sales Manager is different to a traditional Account Manager, but they still fulfill the function of linking the two companies together. Helping the other party and reflecting into their company the needs of the other party, while ensuring the rules are followed and there is a focus on mutual benefit.

Very often, Channel Sales Managers will implement a scorecard or standard report for the Channel Partners. Providing a consistent reporting method for all partners to ensure no surprises with customer issues and sales performance. But, as well as scoring the performance of the Channel Partners, you may also want to monitor and measure the success of the Indirect Channel Sales as a whole, from recruiting to retaining and supporting your customers, their clients.

How many Channel Partners do you want? How long are your Channel Partners staying? How quickly, and at what cost, are they getting up to speed? Where are your Channel Partners coming from? Do you have good product and geographic spread or are there hot spots and blanks?

Once a company has an established Channel Partner, the Channel Sales Manager is responsible for ensuring the Partner performs well. How many deals are they registering and what is their success rate? Often Channel Partners are managed differently to the direct sales team but use the same metrics to measure sales performance such as win rate, sales cycle length, total pipeline numbers, cross-sell and upsell ratios, retention rate, and weighted scorecards.

Other measures can provide insight into how a Channel Partner is performing. Rather than focus exclusively on the sales pipeline and outcomes, the Channel Sales Manager should look for other ways to measure how much the Channel Partners are investing in the partnership and long-term success. How much online, and in-person, training are they undertaking? If the manufacturer provides certification, how many are applying and what is the success rate? How much sales collateral and support are they demanding? What is their Customer Satisfaction score (CSAT)? Is it possible to extract each Channel Partner's CSAT score from the overall total? Is the Channel Partner doing their own CSAT?

Before implementing an Indirect Channel Sales strategy, it is important to determine what type of channel, how many and what limits, or restrictions, or none, should be applied. In Franchising, for example, the rules on who can sell what where are usually strict. For VARs, less so in terms of territories and sectors.

It matters that the manufacturer can identify the best Channel Partners and be able to manage them. Simply taking anyone on board is likely to dilute efforts to manage them which will impact the performance of both parties. It matters also that Channel Partners have the skills and capabilities to deliver the sale and support the sales process to the standards required and be consistent in their support of the supplier company. Often there is a need to invest time in the Channel Partners, to make sure it will deliver results again and again and not be a one-shot win.

A large telecommunications company I was consulting for decided to develop an Indirect Sales Channel for a sector of its customers. The customers were clearly defined by size, spend, geography and products. In total about 150 companies were identified and a Channel Partner was found to manage them.

This was a new way of doing things for the telecommunications company, so they invested a lot in finding the right partner and working closely with them to ensure success. Alone it made no sense to do this as the additional cost of support and time and effort in supporting the partner was more than the cost of managing these accounts in-house. However, it was being used as a pilot for a potentially wider rollout to more regions, more companies and with more products.

I joined the Channel Partner as part of the programme to ensure its success and worked there exclusively for about 18 months. The Channel Partner quickly identified ways of improving the process and how to support its inherited customers as well as implement new sales processes more suited to a small organization rather than a large telecommunications company. They became much more agile and efficient.

Eventually the telecommunications company decided to bring back in-house customers. They applied some of the thinking from the Channel Partner too. The project did not fail, in fact the numbers proved it to be a success. However, the company felt it was not what they wanted to do, there was a change in policy. Staff were offered roles in the parent, but most felt they did not want to work for a large organization so left or stayed with the Channel Partner and moved to new projects.

Just because Indirect Sales Channels can be successful does not mean you should do it.

Indirect Channel Sales success requires commitment by the Channel Sales Partner and the main company itself. It is not enough to find a reseller, of whatever type, provide them some product information, give them a few tools, and let them get on with it. It is also not enough just to manage the relationship on one hand and put into place a raft of metrics on the other.

Good communications and support are vital in the success of the Indirect Sales Channel. Regular meetings with the Channel sales team that build social relationships as well as those that share sales pursuit progress and offer ideas and ways to help are key. Helping with upcoming meetings and presentations and having templated information that can be branded by the reseller. Canned video demonstrations and/or access to a demo facility are all vital tools. In-between all that, an open dialogue and access to allow the salespeople and the management of the Channel sales team access to help whenever they need it.

The most effective Indirect Sales Channels also share CRM systems. Either one provided by the parent organization with ring-fenced areas for each Channel Partner, or access to partner CRMs by the parent for reporting. In many instances, particularly in traditional reseller models, this may be difficult as Channel Partners may be unwilling to share this information. However, for some industry sectors this may be necessary to manage the supply chain. For franchises, it is very often a requirement of the Franchise Agreement to use provided tools or give regular reports in a prescribed format.

For the Indirect Sales Channel, there is the opportunity to adopt a Partner Relationship Management (PRM) system. PRM is more than just software, as CRM is more than just software. It allows companies a way to keep aligned the Indirect Sales Channel business relationships on marketing and sales. Because PRMs look at the entire Sales Funnel it draws in marketing at one end through to sales success and allows for shared reporting and insight through the pursuit. For the parent, it allows extract of their own reports to compare Channel Partners.

To incentivize its use, and some Channel Partners may be reluctant, preferring their own system; requires using it as a tool to share latest updates and information. Leads can be put through the PRM requiring the Channel Partner to use the tool several times a day just to get the information they need, and grab leads before someone else does or before the potential client complains to the parent that they have not had a call back.

A successful Indirect Sales Channel can lead to greater success at lower cost, but with some reduction in net margin on sales of course. It can propel a company forward and allow for rapid growth. The type of channel depends primarily on the product and customer first and the desire of the partner after.

Before embarking on a Channel Strategy, however, it is worth investing the time to decide what type of relationship works best. It is also worth remembering that not every channel type will work and, perhaps, choose more than one. It should also be recognized that different channel types may be more suited to some markets than others, perhaps for logistics or cultural reasons.

Pursuing a channel model may seem like a great way to scale quickly, and it is by no means a commitment for life, but it is a long-term commitment. Channel Partners can be bought out and the channel closed if the company decides to bring back in-house the sales and marketing but, very often there will be a cost.

There is a perception that developing an Indirect Sales Channel is a cheaper way to grow and expand. While it certainly does have financial advantages, this usually only works if done at scale. Having one Channel Partner only still requires management oversight, support, and a team of others to help make it a success.

Developing a Channel Sales Model, ultimately comes down to RoI. The cost of supporting the Indirect Sales Channel, versus the additional revenue and profits generated. This in total form, not just the cost of sale but the cost of supporting the sales, distribution, and customer support. Whether the RoI delivers sufficient versus keeping things in-house needs studying and, while, accelerated growth may be appealing it may not be best for the business. Similarly, Indirect Sales Channels may not be the best approach for the business alone, but it may be an effective tool to accelerate growth and grab market share ahead of the competition.

There are three ways to build sales: Buy, Build, and Borrow. You can buy a company to enter a market or add a new product to sell to your clients. You can build your own sales team and grow the business through marketing and sales. You can develop and build new products and services to sell to customers. You can have a third party do this for you and rely (Borrow) on their sales and marketing to grow the business for you. What works in one market may not work in the next but knowing which of these is best for a business is a key piece of the growth strategy. If the approach is Borrow, for some or all markets, then it matters that you get the right type of Indirect Sales Channel and put into place everything needed to make it a success.

Key Takeaways

The importance of an Online Sales Channels for any business came into sharp focus early in 2020 as the global pandemic forced companies to adapt to restrictions imposed upon them and imposed upon their customers. While B2C saw the brunt of the impact for business and trade, B2B also had to adapt. A greater focus on online marketing and an ability to better serve existing customers and address the interest of potential customers was required. The pandemic accelerated the growth of online retailers, whether in-house or via a third party. It also forced companies to adapt how they supplied customers and how they managed existing relationships. For salespeople, new skills were needed and the honing of existing skills to adapt better to the online world and less face-to-face meetings.

Online Channel Sales offer companies a way to enter markets, expand product offerings, develop synergistic partnerships, and improve cross-sell and upsell. Companies that have developed a robust omnichannel offering where the customer has a seamless experience in buying whether online or in person have seen growth in sales and improved customer satisfaction.

The Online Sales Channel, however, relies on the trust of the buyer. Data breaches and loss of credit and debit card and other personal information impact the trust of the users. Since 2005, the number of data breaches in the United States has grown year on year until 2017 but appears now to be in decline. The number of records exposed starting 2005 has, however, fluctuated between 16 and 222 million save for 2018 when the number of records exposed was ~471 million and now also, apparently in decline.

Customer trust is critical to the success of the Online Sales Channel. However, as the acceleration of Online Sales has continued the chances of an individual being affected is diminishing. In addition, customers are becoming more aware of online safeguards provided or actions they can take and seem less concerned with data breaches. This will further accelerate the use of and therefore the importance of the Online Sales Channel Sale.

Beyond the online options offered, there are a range of indirect sales solutions. Each type of Indirect Sales Channel, or Alternative Sales Channel, provides a different solution for the manufacturing company. It is important to determine what solution is best suited for the needs of each market, each product, and by each manufacturer. Companies can choose multiple Indirect Channel Sale types or could restrict it to only certain products or only for certain markets.

As a new market entry option, the Indirect Sales Channel offers, potentially, a lower risk option financially but perhaps lacks the control over the customer relationship and could pose a threat to brand values. The Indirect Sales Channel can also allow for market segmentation by providing different products in different markets.

The Channel Sale option should not be seen as a hands-off solution to sales. Where direct sales require a team to take to the field consisting of salespeople, marketing, sales support, product specialists, and other skills required, so too does the Indirect Channel Sales model. Support is still required for the product and Channel Managers now take the place of Sales Manager and Account Manager.

The Indirect Sales Channel forms part of the sales solution mix. While it does not suit every industry or product and not every solution is a natural fit, it does provide options. However, these options should not be evaluated and then managed, rather they should be re-evaluated to ensure they still provide a good solution or ones previously dismissed may now offer a good solution.

Management of the Online Channel may be much more a marketing led engagement whereas the Indirect Sales Channel sits firmly between sales and marketing.

CHAPTER 8

Building the Winning Team

The pursuit of a sale through to success is a mix of people, processes, and the product itself. Without a good product, great success cannot be achieved, though many have tried. Without good salespeople, products can sell but not as well, not as efficiently, and not for the margins one would like. Without a process, there is no control over the sale and no insight to give the company the confidence to build more, develop new, and continue with the current.

Of all these, however, people are the single greatest asset to sales success and the area that requires more focus than any other. According to American Major League Baseball player George Herman "Babe" Ruth:

> *The way a team plays determines its success. You may have the greatest bunch of individual stars in the world, but if they don't play together, the club won't be worth a dime.*

All sales begin with marketing, whether it is marketing the brand or marketing the product. All successful sales end with happy customers offering referrals and upsell or cross-sell opportunities. All sales losses lead to new opportunities, win backs, and even referrals! Whether you win and they become your customer, or someone else's is down to the sales team, the leaders, the coaches, and the players. To achieve success takes time, effort, practice, failure, and experimentation.

All sports are played with a set of rules. Selling is no different. But, like all sports teams, they interpret the rules differently and the ones that often have the winning edge play right to the limit of the rules but do so efficiently and consistently. Former Performance Director of British Cycling (1997–2014) Sir David Brailsford implemented a regime of using tiny, marginal gains to improve the success of UK cycling. According to Brailsford:

The whole principle came from the idea that if you broke down everything you could think of that goes into riding a bike, and then improve it by 1 percent, you will get a significant increase when you put them all together.

Brailsford's theory was applied to everything UK cycling did; diet, exercise (on and off the bike), the bicycle itself, aerodynamics, wheels and tires, even the kit the team wore, the course for outdoor cycling and for indoor nature of the track itself. He applied 1 percent not just to the cyclist but to every element of what it took to win. Brailsford focused on every element and every person involved in British cycling, not just the cyclists.

Merely playing as a team is where to start, but it is also only the beginning. In the pursuit of sales, every member of the team has to strive to be better, work harder, work smarter, achieve more, and add more value every day. Whether it is through cold calling, marketing and promotion, product enhancements. or a presentation to a client, a 1 percent improvement in any one of these will make a difference. A 1 percent improvement in all of these consistently will make a huge difference to the eventual winning margin.

Brailsford used the Theory of Marginal Gains to find every advantage possible. Marginal Gains are to be found not just with the people undertaking parts of the process, but with every element that delivers improved sales performance whether that is the technology, systems, and processes involved in and supporting the sales pursuit whether they carry a sales role or not.

In 2004, the UK won two Olympic cycling medals. In 2008 and 2012, the medal tally was 14 medals and 12 medals, respectively. Marginal gains at every level deliver results.

In building a winning sales team, there are no right or wrong answers, there are only ways that work and ways that do not. Ways that work for some customers and for some salespeople. Ways that work now but not in the future and ways that will not work today but may in the future. Ways that will win some games but not others. Every failure is an opportunity to learn. Whether it's failing at recruiting the right people to get the best team or whether it's the process not delivering the right decisions to improve the win rate. A winning team is not just the people; it is the process, the systems, the products and services, the markets, and customers.

Sales, as with products, as with clients, as with the salespeople themselves, is an evolving and changing practice. The teams change, the opposition changes, the rules may even change. The umpire or referee will be different, even the location, the weather and, off the back of a recent win or loss, things will change. Therefore, Sales is perhaps the most exciting place to be in any organization.

Professional sports people relish competition. It teaches them to work harder, train harder, and be more acutely aware of every opportunity. So it is with great salespeople, raising their game to beat the competition.

World and European Champion, World record holder, and Paralympic gold medalist *Danny Crates* sums it up perfectly:

There is no greater feeling than being successful, knowing that all that hard work paid off, and you've nailed it when it's mattered most. Be warned though, there is no worse feeling than knowing you've not nailed it when you could have. Knowing that if you had just given that little bit extra in your preparation, maybe, just maybe the outcome could have been different.

To put together a winning sales team in any company requires an understanding of the process the company wants to follow that is both efficient and effective. That allows the salespeople freedom to pursue but the controls to limit waste. It matches their enthusiasm and excellence with structure and discipline. Aligning all that with the sales process that most customers will ask of and be flexible enough to adapt to different client needs.

Managing each opportunity requires agility on the part of the salesperson, coaching, and guidance from sales management and discipline from the company selling. Remembering too that sometimes the customer is on your side, sometimes not. How often have we accused referees of being impartial or interpreting a rule in a way that advantages one team more than another?

Sales must work with marketing. The influence of marketing, whether online, social media, influencers, opinions and views, customer feedback, or direct advertising all now play a much more significant part in influencing the customer to consider your product. The line between sales and marketing has moved in the direction of marketing. Sales and marketing are two parts of one company objective.

Systems and processes are key to sales efficiency and giving performance insight. Efficiency is the responsibility of all, from the individual salesperson through to the top of the organization. Insight allows better targeting and focus and improves the success outcome ratio. It even points the way to future product development and future marketing strategies.

Building a sales team is an easy thing to do. All the ingredients are well understood and used in countless millions of organizations worldwide. Building an efficient and winning sales team takes a little more effort, and it never stops. Every team is different and none of them stay as they are for long, such are the dynamic levers constantly pulling at the process, the product, the clients, the seller, and the technology.

If you want to build a successful sales team, it requires several building blocks and the will of the team, and the support of the organization. Above all, it requires people with passion and belief, willing to fail, willing to try, and not afraid of the challenges success may bring.

Willingness to fail is a key ingredient in any success. The number of light bulbs Edison tried before he succeeded is apocryphal. *Oprah Winfrey* got fired for being a poor reporter, the *Dyson* vacuum cleaner went through over 1,500 prototypes, and so the list goes on. Every great salesperson has deals they lost that they should not have lost, deals they won that they had no right to (somebody else failed). Failure is a path to success; we learn more from failure than we do if we land on the money every time.

Building a winning team to propel a business forward begins with a strategy and then a plan. A strategy of what you need to achieve and then a timeline of steps and tasks to get there. The goal is clear, to build a solution that works and grows the business through ever better sales success. The plan requires the right people, process, systems, coaches and the right marketing and product or service elements. Failure is not an option for the outcome but failing as you progress is okay.

The Japanese proverb *Nana korobi ya oki* should be part of every sales team mantra. Translated it literally means: "seven falls, eight getting up."

Great salespeople and great Sales Manager do not happen by accident. They invest in their learning and hone their skills. Great sales organizations do not happen by accident, all the right ingredients are brought together to make the whole by the best leaders. All great teams have great players, but players willing to work for the team not for personal glory—that will come anyway. As a team sport, sales also means the Sales Manager must play a role as a leader, as a coach, and even come off the bench to play the game too.

Building a winning sales team requires an efficient sales process that drives effective outcomes; a well-defined product or service offering in the marketplace; a system to manage the process and identify the best pursuits and give insight into winning success; loyal and repeatable customers and advocates; and, above all, the willingness at every level to make it work and have the passion to succeed.

Throughout this book, we have looked at the sales process and how the various components come together from marketing through support. The tools and systems required and the key elements that make up the sinning team. Understanding what each component brings to the team and how it can be turned to advantage is what turns a successful sales team into a great sales performance. Sales do not happen by accident. Excellence does not happen by chance.

To build a winning sales team and go from good to great to exceptional requires an understanding of the team and all the elements and a will to make it happen. A team that has a single dedicated focus: success. To make it happen, everyone must be committed, every day. Failure can come in the smallest corners, and you may not notice until it is too late. Nothing should be left to chance, and no-one should commit less than 100 percent of their ability. Do that, develop a team that wants to win for each other and never stop improving.

Sales really is a team sport more than anything else in business. Play to win and get the best on field and off-field team you can, with the best coaches, the best equipment, and the best gameplan. Be sure to practice, train hard, and remember, after every game there is another game to be played. Great sportspeople can win games, but only great sales teams can win a season and lift the trophy at the end of the year.

References

Adair, J. 1973. *Action Centred Leadership*. New York, USA: McGraw Hill.

Ansoff, H.I. 1957. *Strategies for Diversification*. Harvard Business Publishing, Massachusetts, USA.

Bosworth and Holland. 2004. *Customer Centric Selling*, 1st ed. New York, USA: McGraw Hill.

Branson, R. Founder of Virgin Group.

Cambridge Dictionary. Cambridge University Press, since 1995, Cambridge, UK.

Collins English Dictionary. Harper Collins, since 1979, Glasgow, UK.

Content Marketing Institute (www.contentmarketinginstitute.com).

Customer Insight Group (www.customerinsightgroup.com).

Dağdeviren, O. 2017. *Ait—Çalışan, Anlam Arayan, Yalnızlaşan Şehirli İnsan!* Istanbul, Turkey: Abaküs Kitap.

Danny Crates (www.dannycrates.co.uk).

Deming, W.E. 1993. *The New Economics for Industry, Government, Education*. Cambridge, Massachusetts, USA: MIT Press.

Dixon and Adamson. 2011. *The Challenger Sale: How to Take Control of the Customer Conversation*. Portfolio/Penguin, London, UK.

Dixon, Freeman, and Toman. 2010. *Stop Trying to Delight Your Customers*. Massachusetts, USA: Harvard Business Publishing.

Elias St. Elmo Lewis, USA advertising advocate.

Elop, S. 1963. *We Didn't Do Anything Wrong, But Somehow, We Lost*. Online press conference.

George Herman "Babe" Ruth.

Ghemawat and Siegel. 2011. *Cases about Redefining Global Strategy*. Massachusetts, USA: Harvard Business Publishing.

Goodhart, C. 1975. in an article on Monetary Policy for the UK Government.

Henderson, B. 1968. *Perspectives*. Boston Consulting Group, Massachusetts, USA.

HubSpot, Inc. (www.hubspot.com).

Kapture CRM (www.kapturecrm.com).

Kotler, and Armstrong. 2015. *Principles of Marketing*, 17th ed. Pearson, India.

Marketing Insider Group (www.marketinginsidergroup.com).

Marx, G. 1890–1977. *If You're Not Having Fun, You're Probably Doing Something Wrong*. date unknown, USA.

Maslow, A. 1943. *A Theory of Human Motivation (Psychological Review)*. Washington D.C., USA: American Psychological Association.

Miller and Heiman. 1985. *Strategic Selling*. New York, USA: William Morrow and Company.

Räikkönen, K. 2012. Abu Dhabi Formula 1 Grand Prix, driving for Lotus.

Reichheld, F. 2002. *The One Number You Need to Grow*. Massachusetts, USA: Harvard Business Publishing.

Reichheld, F. 2011. *The Ultimate Question 2.0 (Revised and Expanded Edition): How Net Promoter Companies Thrive in a Customer-Driven World*. Massachusetts, USA: Harvard Business Publishing. Brighton.

Satmetrix Systems, Inc. (www.satmetrix.com).

Shopify (www.shopify.co.uk).

Sir David Brailsford CBE.

Strauss, N. 2014. *The Game and Rules of the Game*. Edinburgh, UK: Canongate.

Strong, E.K., Jr. 1925. *The Psychology of Selling and Advertising*. New York, USA: McGraw Hill.

Superoffice (www.superoffice.com).

Taleb, N.N. 2018. *Skin in the Game*. New York, USA: Random House.

Townsend, W.W. 1924. *Bond Salesmanship*. New York, USA: Henry Holt and Company.

Visier Inc. (www.visier.com).

Companies and Organizations Mentioned in This Book

The 3M Company
7-Eleven Australia Pty Ltd.
The Advertising Standards Authority
Act! LLC
AirBnB Inc.
Alibaba Group
Amazon.com Inc.
Apple Inc.
AuctionWeb
Bain and Company
Bayerische Motoren Werke AG (BMW)
Boston Consulting Group
British Motor Corporation (BMC)
Cadabra, Inc.
Cayan LLC
Chicago Bulls basketball team
The Coca-Cola Company
Colgate-Palmolive Company
The Competition and Markets Authority
Deliveroo Holdings plc
Dyson Ltd.
eBay Inc.
Fairtrade Foundation
Ferrari S.p.A.
Fédération Internationale de Football Association (FIFA)
Finicity Corporation
Flipkart Internet Pvt Ltd.

Ford Motor Company
French Commission for Informatics and Liberty
Fresh & Easy Neighborhood Market
General Electric Company (GE)
General Motor Corporation (GM)
General Motors-Holden
Gillette (part of Procter & Gamble)
Google LLC
Green Dot Corporation
Harley-Davidson, Inc.
Harrods Limited
Harvard Business Review
HubSpot, Inc.
Inter IKEA Systems B.V.
International Cricket Council (ICC)
International Paralympic Committee
Instagram (now part of Facebook, Inc.)
Lego System A/S
LinkedIn
M&Ms (part of Mars, Incorporated)
Marriott International, Inc.
Mars Incorporated
McKinsey & Company
Mercedes-Benz AG
Microsoft Corporation
Miller Heiman Group Limited
Mitsubishi Group
The National Association for Stock Car Auto Racing, LLC (NASCAR)
National Basketball Association (NBA)
Nestlé Nespresso S.A.
NH Hotel Group SA
Nissan Motor Corporation
Nokia Oyj
Numbrs Personal Finance AG
Oracle Systems Corporation
PayPal Holdings, Inc.

PepsiCo, Inc.
Pine Labs Private Limited
Pinterest, Inc.
Group Renault S.A.
Rovio Entertainment Oyj
Royal Automobile Club (RAC)
Salesforce Inc.
Satmetrix Systems
Savoir Beds Ltd.
Shopify Inc.
Siebel CRM Systems Inc. (now part of Oracle Corporation)
Slack Technologies
Snap Inc.
Starbucks Corporation
Suzuki Kabushiki-Gaisha
Tesco plc
TikTok
Toyota Motor Corporation
Trivago N.V.
Twitter, Inc.
Uber Technologies, Inc.
Virgin Group Ltd.
Visa Inc.
Visier Inc.
Washington Wizards basketball team
WeWork
Withers Group Pty Ltd.
Zephyr American Corporation

About the Author

John Fuggles is an experienced sales leader with years of direct hands-on sales experience. He has worked for major multinational organizations in both a sales and sales management. He is also well-regarded consultant advising established and early-stage business as they scale and grow. John recently worked for a charity providing humanitarian aid to Ukraine and is also a Governor of a school. He is also a visiting lecturer at the University of West London. He is married with a family.

Index

www.ingramcontent.com/pod-product-compliance
Lightning Source LLC
Chambersburg PA
CBHW061308220326
41599CB00026B/4784